Landmark
BOOKS

W9-AWJ-746

The Marquis de Lafayette

BRIGHT SWORD FOR FREEDOM

THE
Marquis de Lafayette

Bright Sword for Freedom

By HODDING CARTER

Illustrated by *MIMI KORACH*

RANDOM HOUSE · NEW YORK

TO

Ione Boudreaux Lundy

CONTENTS

The Marquis de Lafayette
BRIGHT SWORD FOR FREEDOM

1

WHY THE VICTOIRE SAILED WESTWARD

On the Sunday morning of April 20, 1777, a freckled-faced, hazel-eyed young nobleman stared anxiously from the deck of the small frigate *Victoire* across the storm-roughened waters of Spain's Bay of Biscay. His reddish hair was powdered in the style of the French court. The young man was not yet twenty.

He had never before made the long, dangerous voyage to the New World of North America. Yet this was the land to whose freedom he had pledged his honor, his great fortune and his sword.

He was shy and awkward. His English was

scanty. Though he came of a heroic family, his own courage had not yet been tested in battle. He and his companions had barely escaped the henchmen of the Bourbon king of France—his king—who, forbidding this madcap journey, had sought to imprison them. His title and long, curious-sounding name would at first make many a plain American rebel smile.

But none of these handicaps bothered the Marquis Marie Joseph Paul Yves Roch Gilbert du Motier de Lafayette, whose friends called him Gilbert and whom the United States, the nation for which he sought to fight, would forever honor as Lafayette, the friend of freedom.

What mattered now was that he and his fellow adventurers were on their way to America despite his family's and his king's determination that they should not leave France. What counted was that they would soon be helping the rebellious American colonies in their war for independence from British tyranny. Important above all, the youthful Lafayette was beginning his lifelong struggle for human liberties against oppressive kings and murderous mobs and, in time, the despotism of a self-made emperor

Young Lafayette stared anxiously across the water.

named Napoleon Bonaparte. That struggle would not end for nearly sixty years, not until the young Marquis was an old man gone to his grave.

And had the *Victoire*—which happily means victory—been overtaken by French or English men-of-war on that desperate voyage and the young

Lafayette forced to return to France, there might not have been a United States of America.

It was as a "very high and very mighty Lord Monseignor" that the infant Lafayette's birth was recorded on September 7, 1757, in the church of the village of Chavaniac. That record was written the day after his birth in the grim, fortress-like castle of Chavaniac, the family seat, deep in the Auvergne district of France. The baby came at a time when it was most lucky, especially in France, to be born a member of the upper classes, and un-lucky to be the child of a poor workingman. To royalty and the nobility, the common man in the France and the Europe of Lafayette's boyhood was no more than a beast of burden. The idle feet of the aristocracy rested on his toil-bent back. Their tax collectors wrung from his labor the millions in gold that were wasted by the king and dukes and barons and marquises and their ladies. The revelry of their banquets, the gay music to which they danced quadrilles and minuets, the scheming chatter of the courtiers of the Bourbons, almost drowned the cries of the starving and oppressed people of France.

Punishment came swiftly to the few sympathizers and sufferers who dared protest aloud, if such protests were heard. Unusual indeed were the noblemen who took pity on the hungry and dreamed of human rights for all men.

Young Gilbert's parents were members of two of the proudest families in all France. They could trace their lineage back to the year 1000, and among their ancestors they counted many brave warriors.

Gilbert's own father, a colonel of Grenadiers, had been killed while fighting the English foe at the Battle of Minden only two years after Gilbert was born. From his grandmother and his aunts and his mother in the remote, cold chateau, he learned of his family's greatness. He may also have learned early that while his own parents were not so wealthy, he would come one day into the fortune which would be left by his grandfather.

But there is no record that he learned from anyone, anywhere in that bleak Auvergne country, the democratic ideas that were later to guide him through life. The very vision of equality and human freedom was foreign to all that his family stood for. Glory, honor, courage, loyalty to family and country, yes. But rights for the common people? Ridiculous!

Yet Gilbert showed early that he thought for himself.

As was the custom among the nobility, he was entered at the age of eleven in the College of Plessis in Paris, the center of French culture. If he followed the usual path of a nobleman, there lay ahead a career as courtier and soldier. Gilbert dreamed of soldiering but not of court life.

When he was first in school, he led a demonstration against the punishment of a comrade who, he thought, was treated unjustly. Soon thereafter when he was asked to write a composition about a perfect horse, he gave indication of the man he would become. His instructor pointed out that the perfect horse was one which was immediately obedient on seeing his rider's whip. That was what the pupils should set down. But Gilbert indignantly described the perfect horse as one which would throw his rider upon seeing the whip. He was awarded the prize, even though this rebellious thought shocked his teacher.

Two years later, when Gilbert was only thirteen, his mother died. Soon thereafter his grieving grandfather died, leaving to young Gilbert one of the greatest fortunes in France with a personal income of 140,000 livres a year. That would equal between two and three million dollars today.

As a thirteen-year-old orphan, Gilbert became a cadet in the regiment of his great-grandfather, the Black Musketeers. The Musketeers were the bodyguards of the king. Now the boy was happy. How he must have gloried in his scarlet and gold uniform, his high jackboots and cocked hat, and the blue mantle embroidered with a cross of silver encircled by flames!

Now he was a soldier of France. His first great day came when he rode up to the king, old Louis XV, after a review of the Black Musketeers, saluted with his sword, and asked if His Majesty had any further orders. His Majesty had none.

Boys became men early in those days. At fourteen Gilbert entered the military academy at Versailles. Before he was fifteen, his guardians decided that it was time for him to marry. And so, negotiations were opened with the brilliant Duke d'Ayen, son of the Duke de Noailles whose family, next to the Royal Bourbons, was the foremost in France. Naturally the Duke was anxious to make a good match for each of his five daughters. The daughter selected for the fourteen-year-old boy was Adrienne, a slender girl of twelve with beautiful eyes. Most properly her mother thought that Adrienne was too young to marry. And so, after quite a family fight, a compromise was arranged. Adrienne and Gilbert would not be married until his education was finished; and in the first year of their marriage Adrienne was not to leave home.

Only two years later, when Gilbert was sixteen and she fourteen, they were married in the private chapel of the de Noailles family palace in Paris. In the midst of all the excitement, King Louis XV died. He was succeeded by his son, dull, simple Louis XVI, and the young, beautiful and spendthrift queen, Marie Antoinette.

With a new king at Versailles, the Duke and Duchess d'Ayen decided it was time for their young son-in-law and his bride to be seen at court.

The family was in a favored position. Gilbert's father-in-law, the Duke d'Ayen, immediately was appointed commander of the King's bodyguard. Young Gilbert was commissioned a captain in the Noailles Dragoons, the family's own picked soldiers. That fall the Duke opened his magnificent mansion at Versailles, where rose the pleasure palace of the King. That winter the Duchess presented her son-in-law and his child wife at court.

It is almost impossible for us to imagine today the glitter, the waste and the wickedness of court life in Bourbon France. Blonde, young Marie Antoinette dominated the spectacular gatherings of the nobility and the lesser hangers-on and seekers-after-favor. They danced, they drank, they flirted. They amused themselves with masked balls and costly banquets and private theatricals. The idling nobles caroused and dueled and made love to the ladies of the court. And always the Queen's cry was for money, money, more money—money to be taken from the very lifeblood of her subjects. One day she and Louis would pay a terrible price for their folly. But that lay ahead.

The young Marquis de Lafayette had little liking for court life. He was a quiet and serious boy, not given to light behavior. At court he felt bored and out of place. He did not like to drink, and heavy drinking was fashionable. And once the Queen, dancing in a minuet in which he was a not very graceful member, laughed at a false step he made. He never forgot the insult, and he never became a real courtier.

Gilbert was also rebelling against the wastefulness of the life to which he had been born. At Versailles there were two thousand servants. Each year the Queen was spending six million livres to feed her friends and her court. All the while people went hungry, and this shamed young Lafayette.

To his happiness, his wide-eyed little wife liked court life no better than did he. She was content to be Gilbert's marquise and to try to keep up with his studious interests. She did not protest when her stubborn young husband made an intentionally rude remark that displeased the King and ruined his chances for courtly advancement. Clearly he was determined to avoid being driven into an honorary post at court.

And so matters stood, when, in the summer of 1775, the course of Gilbert's life was fixed. For it was then that he learned of the Colonial rising in America. It was a story which fired his imagination more than any other in all the seventy-seven years that he would live.

The eighteen-year-old guardsman was with his

The French nobility enjoyed costly balls and banquets.

regiment in the frontier garrison city of Metz. There, strangely enough, he received from a liberal-minded young Englishman his first account of the great George Washington and the rebels who followed him. The spokesman was the Duke of Gloucester, brother of the English king, George III.

The Englishman and Frenchman sat next to each other at a dinner. Gloucester talked sympathetically about the American revolutionists. Right was on their side, he said. Young Lafayette asked many questions. Before the night had ended, he had made up his mind to go to the New World to fight for the liberty of men whose land he had never seen, whose tongue he could not speak and whose very cause had been so recently unknown to him.

But the need for human liberty he could understand. And an American victory would mean a double triumph. The rights of free men would be won; England would be humbled. And France would be avenged for her defeat in the Seven Years' War, which had ended only twelve years before and in which his father had died.

We cannot go far into the intrigues and plotting that surrounded the cause of America in

Europe. Some plain people, students, and great thinkers were challenging the idea that kings had God-given special rights; but there were few among the statesmen and rulers of Europe who had true sympathy for the American cause itself. Most of them thought our Declaration of Independence was full of dangerous notions.

Yet there were many who wanted to punish England, a powerful nation which seemingly could not be defeated. That is why more than four-fifths of America's gunpowder and arms were supplied, more or less in secret, by the governments of France and Spain in the early years of the American Revolution. It was a means of striking a blow at England.

But to Gilbert the cause of freedom came first. Determined to fight for the Americans, he joined forces with a tough, brave, old soldier of fortune who also wanted to fight for America. This man was a solid, dependable German who called himself the Baron Johann de Kalb because that title seemed necessary to get ahead among the French nobility. However, he was actually just plain Johann Kalb.

At first the stubborn Americans were considered silly. But as the months passed, they won the admiration of the people of France, and especially of Paris, by the fight they were putting up.

And so it was that Silas Deane, one of the three American commissioners sent to Paris to enlist aid for the American cause, was besieged by requests from adventurous young Frenchmen for commissions in the American army.

Many wanted pay. A few had no thought of personal profit, among them the Marquis de Lafayette. His closest comrade was de Kalb, who, because he had no great fortune and also because he was a professional soldier, expected some reward. To both of them Deane held out hope for commissions as generals in the American army.

There followed a difficult period of waiting. Paris was a city of intrigue, and the young Lafayette was no low schemer. He had only one aim—to fight for freedom. He, de Kalb and their handful of associates kept their plans secret until, at last, they despaired of success. Then Lafayette's brother-in-law, the young Duke de Noailles, went to his powerful family head and sought permission for him and Lafayette to set sail. Angrily, the Duke d'Ayen forbade the adventurers to go to America.

But Lafayette did not give up. He decided he would go, with or without anyone's consent. He determined to buy a vessel on which he and a chosen group would embark for America. The party included de Kalb, a number of friends and a staff, including two valets—considered the least number a titled gentleman could do with.

Not until February, 1777, did de Kalb finally secure, through Commissioner Deane, the enrollment of the Marquis de Lafayette and himself as major generals in the army of the revolutionary Americans. A major general and not yet twenty, not even yet tried in battle! It seems incredible today. But Deane was no fool. The young Marquis was a representative of two of the leading families of France. His in-laws were powerful at court. If his sincere devotion to the cause of America could be put to good use, who could tell what would follow?

This was a bold scheme. But for Gilbert it was no scheme at all, only an opportunity to fight for liberty. During his long wait, he went to London where he was welcomed sensationally. He did not hide his pro-American feelings. Instead, he boasted of his sympathies, and among many young and liberal Englishmen he found kindred fellows. He was even presented to the hated King George III. But despite an official invitation, his honor forbade him to inspect an English military expedition that was setting sail for America. As an appointed major general in the army opposing England, he could not do this even in secret.

Soon Gilbert returned to France and made ready. His worried wife didn't know of his plans for secret departure. For three days he hid at de Kalb's little house near Paris. Then on March 16, 1777, he and de Kalb set out in Gilbert's own coach for Bordeaux where the frigate, *Victoire,* which he had personally chartered, waited. His own identity as a passenger had been concealed. He traveled in disguise.

But now incautious enthusiasm disturbed the well-laid plans. Gilbert had told several friends of his goal. Of course, the secret came out. Just as he was boarding the small boat which was to take him to the *Victoire,* a letter arrived from a friend. The French court was aroused. His father-in-law was exceedingly angry. He would surely be arrested and brought back to Paris, not as a political prisoner but as proof that the King's will and that of his own father-in-law were supreme.

But rebel Gilbert would not be halted. The *Victoire* sailed to Spanish waters and hid in the Bay of Los Pasajes. Even there they were found out. A letter from the King himself arrived, commanding the fleeing Marquis to go into exile in Italy and Sicily for ten months.

This meant that Lafayette was all but under arrest. Back to Bordeaux he went. He found no support from any of his relatives. The King was very angry. He was threatening prison for Gilbert. So the Marquis pretended that he had decided to abandon his adventure.

Then he learned that the reason the King had ordered him not to quit France was because of his father-in-law's complaint. The whole of Paris, he was told, had applauded his daring. Thereupon Gilbert decided that the later silence of the King and his advisors meant that he could leave. It was a wrong assumption but a worthy one. With the King's men after him, the defiant Marquis set sail on that April Sunday in 1777 from the port of Los Pasajes and put out into the Bay of Biscay. Every French ship which could be reached by royal order would be under notice to arrest him.

All day and evening he and his small company watched the Spanish cliffs vanish. The boy marquis who had left behind him an angry monarch, a no less irate family and a sad and unbelieving wife, wrote that he was "oppressed by the appalling loneliness of the sea at evening, and troubled by the thought of what he had done." He asked himself whether it was all worth it.

Try to imagine the difficulties of a fugitive noble, hunted by the rulers of his own country and of England, uncertain of the reception he would receive in the rebellious colonies, too seasick for dreams of glory. On the long and tedious voyage he studied English and the science and art of war. Always he or his companions kept a lookout for English warships, long after they had left pursuing French vessels behind.

From cold March until the end of May their troubles grew. Continually, Lafayette wrote to the wife who he hoped would forgive him. In one of these letters he made a far-seeing comment. "To America," he said, "I bring my sincerity and my good will; no ambition or selfish interest. In striving for my glory I strive for their happiness. I hope that in my favor you will become a good American. It is a sentiment made for all virtuous hearts; the happiness of Americans is intimately bound up with the happiness of humanity. She is going to become a cherished and safe asylum of virtue, of tolerance, of equality and of peaceful liberty. . . ."

These were a prophet's words!

On Friday, June 13, 1777, after fifty-four days of perilous voyage, the *Victoire* dropped anchor in a South Carolina bay. The captain had missed the Port of Charleston, South Carolina, but at any rate this was American soil.

The French Marquis knelt on the sands when they reached land.

"I will conquer or perish with the Americans' cause," he swore.

Then the party learned from four frightened Negroes where they were. Charleston was fifty miles away, but in this plantation country they were among friends. The tired Lafayette was made welcome by Major Benjamin Huger, whose son, now a toddler, would seek nearly twenty years later to free Lafayette from a European prison.

Gilbert and de Kalb procured horses from Major Huger and almost immediately set out for Charleston. They made the journey in two days. But their companions, who were forced to travel by foot, arrived three days after them, worn out and famished. And here at Charleston the Frenchmen had a rude shock. The people of Charleston had decided that they had seen enough of the French for a while. The trouble was that the city was full of the ragtag and bobtail of the French West Indies and debt-ridden French officers who wanted to sell their services. Lafayette and his friends were jeered at in the streets.

But with the arrival of the *Victoire* at Charleston, the story of the strange Marquis became known. The Lafayette volunteers were cheered everywhere and welcomed royally. The enthusiastic Frenchman charmed everyone. He in turn fell equally in love with America.

"They are as kind as my enthusiasm has been able to represent them," he wrote Adrienne. "The simplicity of manners, the desire to please, the love of country and of liberty, the delightful equality that reigns everywhere; the richest man and the poorest are on a level. The resemblance in their ways of thinking to my own, my love for glory and for liberty, is striking."

Then the Frenchmen found out that they had been tricked by the French captain of the *Victoire*. They had expected to sell the ship and her cargo for money enough for their journey to Philadelphia to meet George Washington and join the American army. But the captain presented a financial note which the Marquis had hastily signed without reading. Under its terms the vessel and its cargo were to return to France to be sold, and the captain paid from the proceeds. The Marquis found that he could not borrow enough money in Charleston to provide ship passage north, though he did raise a few thousand dollars on his own signature.

Much disheartened, the voyagers set out overland on June 25, 1777. They must have seemed rather imposing, at that. One of the Marquis' two valets, dressed as a French hussar, rode ahead. Next came a large open carriage in which sat the Marquis and

Johann de Kalb. Beside the carriage rode the other servant, and behind them rocked several carriages with the rest of the party.

But the Frenchmen looked neither gay nor brilliant when they arrived in Philadelphia thirty-two days later. Their carriages had broken down on the wilderness trails and had been abandoned four days after they had left Charleston. Most of their horses had died. Some of their baggage had been dis-

Next came the Marquis and de Kalb in an open carriage.

carded and almost all of the rest stolen. They had
spent nearly five terrible weeks, tortured by heat
and mosquitoes and flies, sometimes without food.
Most of them suffered from fever. Only through
Lafayette's prodding and encouragement had they
made the difficult journey.

"We must do it," he had said over and over.
"It is for the cause of liberty."

2

A MEETING WITH WASHINGTON

Throughout the arduous journey to Philadelphia, young Gilbert and his companions had comforted themselves by talking of the friendly reception which surely awaited them in the revolutionary capital. But when they arrived they suffered an unbelievable disappointment.

After making themselves as presentable in their worn clothing as they could, they went at once to call, not on Washington, but on the president of the American Congress. At his offices they were rudely told by a secretary to come back the next day.

Bewildered, they returned to their lodgings. Next morning they returned. To their amazement and anger, they were angrily warned by a member of Congress that they were considered as no-goods and money-seeking adventurers. The discouraged Frenchmen did not then know that they had been betrayed by an unfriendly fellow countryman who had come over earlier to fight for the Americans for a price, and who was afraid that Lafayette and his men would replace him in the Americans' eyes. The bitter French aristocrats and hard-bitten Johann de Kalb were on the verge of giving up in disgust.

Then Lafayette, without saying a word to anyone, sent an amazing note to the president of Congress. It was a stroke of unselfish genius.

"After the sacrifices that I have made," he wrote, "I have the right to demand two favors. One is to serve at my own expense. The other is to begin my service as a volunteer."

This was a far cry from the commissioning in France of a nineteen-year-old Frenchman as a major general in the American Army, with an agreement to pay him and his fellows for their military services. The American Congressman decided to reconsider. After all, Lafayette was a member of a notable French family, and his wish to serve America for love of liberty and without reward was obvious from the generous tone of his letter. Members of Congress reasoned that he could win friends abroad for the American cause.

There followed an immediate about-face by the Americans. Again Lafayette was offered a commission as major general. But he must serve without pay and, at the beginning, without command of troops. Gilbert was elated once more. What did a rich French nobleman care for money? He had plenty of his own at home. And if he won the rank of major general, command of troops would certainly follow. With his feelings greatly soothed, Gilbert read, four days later, a unanimous resolution by Congress.

"Whereas the Marquis de Lafayette, out of his great zeal to the cause of liberty, in which the United States are engaged, has left his family and connections and at his own expense come over to offer his services to the

United States without pension or particular allowance, and is anxious to risk his life in our cause—

"Resolved that his services be accepted, and that in consideration of his zeal, illustrious family and connections, he have rank and commission of Major General in the Army of the United States."

With the copy of the resolution came the scarf of a major general in the American army.

By now a great British fleet under Lord Howe had appeared off Delaware. The Englishman had decided to move his army into Pennsylvania. Washington had urgent need to confer with his generals. The day after Gilbert received his commission he was invited to a dinner given by the commander in chief.

The exuberant youth went in great excitement to meet the man whom he would soon cherish as a father no less than he would respect him as a military leader. As he entered the banquet room, he saw at the other end of the banquet hall a gigantic figure dressed in the blue and buff uniform of the Continental Army, his hair white with powder, his face reddened by many years of out-door living. Later Lafayette recalled that he recognized him almost immediately, by "the majesty of his countenance and his tall form."

In the presence of the American whom he had already worshiped almost idolatrously, young Lafayette was afraid. But the warmth of Washington's welcome put him at his ease almost immediately. And with that meeting began a rare and lasting attachment, one which was to be of untold benefit to the American cause and the ever-lasting cause of human freedom everywhere. What a contrast they must have formed: the ungainly, nervous French noble who had never known his own soldier father, and the towering, mature American of forty-nine, who had never fathered a son.

Before he resisted his British monarch, George III, Washington's only experience of war had been in fighting the French and their Indian allies in England's behalf; and in that same Seven Years' War in which Washington defended Britain's colonies in America, young Gilbert's father had been killed by British artillerymen in Europe.

Now they would serve together under the flag of the rebel nation. They were as different in their dispositions, for the most part, as they were in age and nationality. Washington was patient, self-disciplined, serious and always in control of himself, a wealthy squire of the New World, as much an aristocrat in his frontier country as was the young Lafayette in France. And the noble volunteer, his French temperament driving him often to rash decisions, was warmhearted, impetuous, and, in time, even more dedicated to some of the more advanced principles of eighteenth-century democracy than was George Washington himself.

But both had in common complete honesty, an unchallengeable courage and full devotion to the American cause. These characteristics would carry them through the years to come when less strong-willed and consecrated men would have long since surrendered.

Throughout that first meal Lafayette rarely took his eyes off General Washington. The General was undoubtedly conscious of the hero-worshiping Marquis' behavior. When they returned to the parlor, he made sure to converse with the French nobleman and compliment him on his willingness to give up his easy life for the cause of America.

"I cannot promise you the luxuries of a court,"

Washington told Gilbert. "But I know that as an American soldier you will strive to adjust yourself to your new character and to submit with grace to the customs and privations of a republican army."

Neither could have known that night just how great those privations would be before the ultimate victory.

And then the General made the French volunteer's happiness complete with an invitation to in-

Lafayette went with Washington to review the troops.

spect with him next day the fortifications of the
Delaware and to stand beside him as he reviewed
the Continental troops.

That next day was an eye-opener for the former
lieutenant of the Black Musketeers. As for the
fortifications, they seemed skillfully enough con-
structed. The Continental Army did have the
services of some skilled European military engi-
neers. But the Army itself was something else
again. Gilbert could hardly believe his eyes when
he saw the American soldiers at their camp about
five miles north of Philadelphia, spread out on the
hot and dusty plain. Here were gathered 11,000
Continentals, mostly ragged, disheveled civilian
soldiers. Some were even without shoes. Many of
them were clad in the loose-hanging shirts of the
backwoodsman or the rough homespun of the small-
town artisan and the unmilitary garb of the city
dweller. No two were alike in uniform or in
military tactics.

Gilbert's surprise must have been reflected in his
face.

"We are rather embarrassed to show ourselves
to an officer who has just left the army of France,"
Washington said in friendly apology for his troops.

"I am here, sir, to learn and not to teach," young Lafayette answered.

That answer meant much to Washington. So many of the foreign-born soldiers who had offered to serve him did not believe they could learn anything from the Americans, not even the meaning of the spirit of liberty itself.

But there were flies in the eager volunteer's ointment. One was that although he kept prodding, as strongly as he could, for troops of his own to command, nothing happened. In fact, his commander in chief seemed a little irritated that he should continue to ask.

Even worse was his failure to have his companions of the *Victoire* enrolled in the American Army. Congress paid no attention to them. They were living in cheap rooming houses, hoping against hope. Lafayette himself could do nothing with Congress, nor did an appeal to Washington get any results. He was tempted to hand in his own commission and return to France with his friends. But he had already accepted a high rank in the American Army. To turn back might be misinterpreted as cowardice. He stayed on.

Eventually, experienced Johann Kalb won his commission, but not before many harsh words and threats to sue the Colonials. A few of the others who came with Gilbert also eventually found their way into the army.

More attention should be paid by history to fearless Johann de Kalb who called himself the Baron de Kalb. Whatever else he was, he was a fighting man. And as a fighting man he was to die at Camden, South Carolina, in 1780. There he tried to halt the sad rout of an American force under General Horatio Gates. Only Johann de Kalb and a few of his men fought to the end. His courage and that of the handful under him almost saved the day; and he gave his life for America on that Southern battlefield, bleeding from eleven wounds.

On August 20, 1777, Lafayette became an official member of General Washington's military family. That day he joined the army in its camp on the old York Road in Bucks County, Pennsylvania. The very next day he listened quietly at his first council of war, while Washington and the older generals discussed gravely the movements of Admiral Howe's fleet. All knew that a new test of arms was at hand.

In Philadelphia were many Tories, citizens who

were loyal to the English crown. Washington determined to remind them of his strength. So on August 24th he led his army into Philadelphia. The tattered rank and file were alike only in that each man wore green leaves in his hat or on his hatless head—leaves symbolic of the American tree of liberty. At Washington's side rode Lafayette, the romantic young Frenchman, who now saw in these men the certainty of freedom. But he and his loved commander would know many a weary, heartsick and despairing hour before that freedom was won.

Already Howe and the British redcoats were knocking at the doors of Philadelphia.

3

THE DARK HOURS

We wonder today how the ragged, untrained, poorly armed Colonials fought for more than six years against British regulars, German hirelings and the well-equipped American Tories who battled their fellow Americans in behalf of a distant king. Certainly professional military men must have marveled during the American Revolution.

The American militiamen were lacking woefully in discipline. The British foemen were well equipped, and so disciplined that they would too often march without flinching to certain death. The Americans always suffered from a shortage of arms, ammunition, uniforms, food and medicine. The British had a navy which could land not only troops but supplies. Great Britain had ample funds to pursue a war. The Colonials had almost no navy except for raiders, and no treasury. Nearly one-third of the people of America were hostile to the Revolution.

On the other hand, the American rebels did have the sympathy of leading Englishmen. Britain was fighting the war at a great distance from the homeland. She had other and stronger enemies near by, and the stubborn British military refused to adopt tactics suited to frontier fighting.

Also in the Colonials' favor was their acquaintance with firearms. They were pioneers, used to rifle and knife. They were fighting for their homes and freedom on territory that they knew. Many of their military leaders had learned much during the Seven Years' War, which Americans had named the French and Indian War. In George Washington they had an inspired and immortal leader and, in their determination to be free, an unyielding cause. By no means least, they had the Marquis de Lafayette who, in his person and as a symbol of French support, would be worth thousands of men to the Americans.

But in the early autumn of 1777 many an

American heart was heavy with fear. The British
fleet had landed 18,000 veteran troops only fifty
miles from Philadelphia. These invincibles were
marching on the capital. Skirmishing between the
redcoats and the men in homespun began early in
September. And on September 9th, falling back
before the advancing invaders, Washington crossed
Brandywine Creek. That night he took possession
of the hilly ground on its east bank. During the
tense evening, Gilbert confided to friends his belief that he would be wounded in the coming
battle, his first trial of arms.

He slept little that night. He was up and in the
saddle at dawn, riding along the American lines
beside the calm and silent Washington. It took only
a glance at the sad, set face of his commander to
make him realize that Washington knew that a
crisis was near.

The Americans were doomed to defeat. Howe
had carefully planned his attack. The principal
British drive would be directed against General
Sullivan on the American right. There Lafayette
waited. Through his spyglasses he watched the
opening of the battle. Before him the Americans,
confronted with the gleaming British bayonets,

broke and ran. In an attempt to stop their retreat, Gilbert leaped from his horse and struck at the frightened, undisciplined men.

Soon the oncoming British were only twenty yards away from him. Someone touched him and pointed to his leg. Blood streamed from a wound. His friend and aide, Major Gimat, who had come to America with him, helped him to mount his horse. But Gilbert did not retire at once. Finally, when he was weak from loss of blood and caught in the retreating mass of Americans, he was carried along, still vainly trying to halt the retreat and renew the fight. At a bridge near Chester, Pennsylvania, Washington found him. Even in the heat of a battle, the commander in chief had great concern for his young ally. He ordered that Gilbert be taken away to safety.

"Treat him as though he were my son," he commanded the Continental doctors.

Gilbert lay that night at Chester with many other wounded Americans. The next day he was removed to Philadelphia. There he heard that his commander had commended him officially for bravery. Gilbert had been true to his father's memory.

"Treat him as though he were my son," said the General.

But his own achievements, his courage in the face of the first enemy he had ever confronted, were as nothing to the fact of the American defeat. The Americans had suffered 1,000 casualties, the British only half that number. The wounded Marquis was removed to Bethlehem, a settlement of peace-loving religious Germans from Moravia, now crowded with refugees. The gentle Moravian settlers chided him for his warlike spirit. They tried to persuade him that non-resistance was the only course for Christian people. But Gilbert paid no attention to these kindly urgings. He wanted to have another chance at the enemy.

As the weeks passed and his wound healed, his spirits fell, and not only because of the American defeat. He had not been put in charge of troops. He was lonely for his wife and homesick. Had George Washington not been determined to keep this youth whose loyalty and courage so heartened him, the Marquis might have left America then.

The lowest ebb of the Revolution had come. Now began a long winter ordeal for the Americans. On October 3rd they had again been defeated at the Battle of Germantown. Seven hundred Americans were wounded or dead, and 400 others taken prisoner, as against British losses of a little more than 500. Enemies within his own ranks were plotting against Washington, and efforts were even made to enlist the support of Lafayette against his leader. The badly beaten Americans evacuated Philadelphia and retreated to Valley Forge, northwest of Germantown and less than thirty miles from Philadelphia itself.

What a contrast that winter between the opposing forces! Philadelphia was bright and gay. The British sympathizers—the Tories—were many; and they entertained the British officers with grand balls and theater parties and card playing. It was just as well for the Americans at Valley Forge that the British under Sir William Howe were enjoying themselves so much. Sir William figured that he could end the war almost any time, so why do it in the cold of winter? By spring the Rebels would have given up and gone home, he thought. And so, instead of crushing Washington's little force as he so easily could have, Sir William enjoyed himself.

His fellow general, Lord Cornwallis, was less peaceably inclined. Across the Delaware he was raiding farms in New Jersey. Washington ordered General Greene, his ablest commander, to follow Cornwallis and nip at his heels. It was November and Gilbert's wound had not yet fully healed; but he begged to be allowed to accompany the expedition. Washington agreed. Greene was delighted, and off the Marquis went, still limping a little.

Now he was to win his first command and his first victory. Put in charge of a little detachment of some three hundred cavalrymen and militiamen, he went ahead of the main American force to study the British positions. While his men concealed themselves in some woods, the Marquis boldly dismounted and limped out alone in plain sight of the entrenched foe. These were Hessians, German mercenary soldiers, hired by the British.

Gilbert ordered an attack upon the strong outpost; and soon the cross-belted Germans were fleeing before Gilbert and his Americans. That did it. He was given his choice of any division which had no commander. He chose a Virginia division of light infantry. Washington was a Virginian.

But this minor victory over the Hessians was almost the last hopeful news in that killing winter at Valley Forge. The dreadful months were brightened for Lafayette only by word on December 19th that in long-ago July his second child, another girl, was born. Poor Adrienne herself had been very ill and was suffering from great anxiety; for she had not learned that her husband had arrived safely in America until well after the birth of little Anastasie. Meanwhile the French, English and Dutch newspapers had been filled with sensational stories about the young French hero, some even reporting that he had been killed.

Adrienne would have been almost as anxious had she known the conditions under which her husband was living in the Pennsylvania wintertime.

His new division was hardly the size of a regiment. Enlistments had all but ceased, and desertions from the Continental Army were mounting. Troops and officers lived in crude log huts which barely sheltered them against the winter rigors. Many of the men went barefoot in the snow, and the surgeons were busy amputating frozen feet. Even commanding officers went about wrapped in woolen blankets. Some days the troops actually had not a single meal, and often there was only one ration issued a day.

Gilbert marveled at their endurance. "The patience and fortitude of officers and soldiers was a continual miracle that each moment renewed," he recollected later. That miracle could not have been accomplished without Washington, whose strong will kept alive the Revolution. The great leader found comfort and understanding in the hardy French nobleman, now just twenty, who so steadfastly stood by him and America.

The troops adored Gilbert. He was known as "the soldier's friend," for he shared every hardship and refused any special treatment. He lived in a tent, as did Washington, until huts could be built for all of the soldiers, though the thermometer read below zero. He even learned to eat salt pork, hardtack and hominy.

That winter the Revolution almost ended. Congress was divided into angry factions. The conspiracy to ruin Washington was gaining ground. The country was plagued with worthless paper money and skyrocketing prices. Unpatriotic speculators made high profits. Trading with the enemy was common. Congress was not willing to levy taxes, for it knew they could not be collected from people who were losing heart.

In New York Sir Henry Clinton was living with his thousands of British troops as luxuriously as was Sir William Howe in Philadelphia. Across the river from New York a few hundred Continental soldiers, as ragged and desperate as their brothers at Valley Forge, kept a semblance of an army together. Altogether Washington could count only 5,000 forlorn soldiers.

In only one area, northern New York, had American arms met with success. In a bloody campaign American frontiersmen were fighting not only the regular British troops but also fierce Mohawk Indians and Loyalists. There General John Burgoyne had been surrounded at Saratoga, New York, and forced to surrender with 5,700 men.

The men who plotted against Washington were led by General Horatio Gates and Colonel Thomas Conway, an Irishman who had previously served in the French army. They sought to use young Lafayette as a tool. They wooed him with flattery. But before they got very far, Lafayette read some intercepted letters between Gates and Conway. From them he learned of the scheme to ruin Washington. His idol was in danger.

Lafayette wrote a long letter to Washington expressing his loyalty and sorrow and disillusion. "I am now fixed to your fate," he ended, "and I shall follow it and sustain it as well by sword as by all means in my power."

Part of the plot was to separate Lafayette from Washington. He had been offered command of an expedition to invade Canada. He accepted gladly. But when he reached Albany, New York, where the invasion expedition was supposed to assemble, he found he had been tricked. Only a few freezing men were there, without adequate food or clothes or weapons. He protested the ridiculous situation, and Congress recalled him.

Lafayette shared the hardships of Valley Forge.

Back to Valley Forge he went, but not before he had won some Oneida Indians to the American cause. He was appalled at the ferocity of the Indians who for a few "geegaws and a keg of rum from the English" were ravaging and murdering along the western frontier.

By early April Lafayette and de Kalb, who had accompanied him on the New York expedition, had returned to Valley Forge. The treasonable Conway was drummed out of the Army, and seriously wounded in a duel with one of Washington's loyal generals.

With the warm, green springtime, the condition and the spirits of the Continental troops improved vastly. Under the direction of a stern Prussian drill-master, the Baron von Steuben, who had volunteered to serve with the American forces, new recruits were being turned into well-trained soldiers. The rations had improved under the supervision of the devoted General Greene.

And on May 2, 1778, came word of the most significant and welcome event of the whole war. The Americans learned that early in the new year France, which the previous December had recognized the independence of the United States, had entered into an alliance with the warring nation. The alliance, it was agreed, was to become effective only if war broke out between France and Britain. But everyone knew that another war between these ancient enemies would not be long in coming. And come it did, on the seventeenth of June, when French and British naval forces clashed.

There were old and new reasons for this fortunate treaty. The French statesmen and military leaders saw in it a means of depriving Britain of her American colonies and possibly regaining France's own lost holdings. But, without doubt, the presence of Lafayette with the American forces, and his role as the hero of the New World, hastened the French decision and brought for it the support of the people of France.

Throughout the Colonies the patriots stirred with new hope. France was their ally. France, they said joyfully, had a powerful navy and a large, well-led army. Together, the Americans and the French would drive the British into the sea.

The first good augury was the evacuation of Philadelphia by the British. The redcoats, too, had heard that a French fleet was on the way.

4

THE ROAD TO YORKTOWN

This story of Lafayette cannot include a full account of the American Revolution. The fight for independence had begun in April, 1775, on the village green in little Lexington, Massachusetts, more than two years before Lafayette reached the embattled continent. The final peace treaty was not signed until September 3, 1783.

The struggle was not easily won. In the years after the alliance with France, the Americans suffered reverses as menacing to freedom's cause as had been the dreadful winter at Valley Forge. They won notable victories and were almost crushed by new defeats. They were plagued by political cowardice and short-sightedness. Even Washington despaired time and again. From the Canadian border to South Carolina hundreds of men and women and children, loyal to the Revolution, were massacred by Indians and Tories. The American cause produced heroes aplenty: "Mad Anthony" Wayne, Nathaniel Greene, Francis Marion and Andrew Pickens, Isaac Shelby, Daniel Morgan, Lighthorse Harry Lee, George Rogers Clark, John Paul Jones, the sea raider, and many another. But it also counted its cowards and double-dealers and shameful traitors, of whom Lafayette had full and sorrowful knowledge.

Gilbert never faltered in the darkest hours. His six years of service in the American cause were interrupted only by a brief, triumphant visit to France. In those years he had adventures enough to satisfy a hundred fighting men. In the jubilant celebration at Valley Forge, honoring the alliance with France, the Marquis was almost as warmly cheered and admired as was Washington. And in France, Voltaire, the daring thinker and critic of kings, gave credit to Lafayette for the entry of France into the war against England. He described

him as the hero of the New World and expressed
the hope that he himself would live long enough
to salute in Lafayette "the liberator also of the
old world."

But Gilbert's happiness at the turn of events was
sadly marred by the news, at almost the same
time, of the death of his older daughter, Henriette,
seven months before.

The Marquis seemed to have a charmed life.
By now he had become an especial target of the
British. They were determined to capture the volunteer foeman whom they described contemptuously
as "the boy." Early in the summer of 1778 the
British General Clinton thought that Lafayette's
capture was sure. Spies told him that Gilbert, at
the head of 2,000 troops, could be surrounded by
surprise. At the time Gilbert was on a mission to
learn what Clinton intended to do in Philadelphia.
Hastily Clinton set out with more than 10,000 men
to trap the Marquis at Barren Hill. But Gilbert
skillfully eluded his pursuers, slipping through two
advancing redcoat columns by a steep and little
used pathway to the Schuylkill River. He led his
troops across the Schuylkill without losing a man,
just ahead of the foiled enemy.

Soon thereafter his life and, what was more important to him, his reputation, were endangered because of the treason or stupidity of General Charles Lee. Lee was a turncoat Englishman who served in the American army. Charles Lee was no relative of the Lees of Virginia. His trickery or cowardice at the Battle of Monmouth turned an almost certain victory into near defeat; for he gave conflicting orders, commanded men to retreat when they were holding fast and so disorganized the Continentals that only a desperate charge by Anthony Wayne and the personal valor of Greene and Lafayette saved the day. When Washington learned at the height of battle of Lee's behavior, he lost his temper publicly for the only time during the war. He roundly cursed Lee and removed him from his command. But the damage had been done.

Soon thereafter the first French fleet arrived. Gilbert was beside himself with joy. He called upon Admiral d'Estaing on August 4th and was given command of the initial landing party of French infantry. Soon thereafter the French fleet skirmished with British men-of-war. The Marquis cheered wildly as he saw the Britishers running away from the ships of France.

The arrival of these allies, however, was marred by old enmities between the French and the Colonists who had once been English subjects. Gilbert was saddened by the bitterness of the quarrel between officers and men on both sides. So aroused was he that at one point he challenged the American General Sullivan to a duel for his contemptuous comments about France. After the failure of a French expedition against Newport, Rhode Island, Washington intervened in the growing quarrel and relationships improved.

Gilbert helped as a peacemaker, but he was disappointed that victory seemed no nearer. He tried to persuade Washington to organize an expedition of French and Americans against Canada. Washington refused. Gilbert then decided to return to France, not permanently, but to see his family and to work at court for the American cause.

It had been many, many months since the *Victoire* had sailed from the Bay of Biscay. Now was a good time to return. Lafayette's temper had been strained to the breaking point, and his spirit

had been saddened by quarrels, political manipu-
lations and delays in prosecuting the war. Congress granted him indefinite leave, voted to have
Benjamin Franklin, the American Minister to
France, present him an elaborate sword after he
reached home, and placed a fine new 36-gun
frigate, the *Alliance*, at his disposal for the voyage.

The sailing was delayed because of Gilbert's
illness. He almost died of what was described as
an inflammatory malady. And on the voyage itself
his life was twice in grave danger. Winter gales
were raging, and the *Alliance* soon sprang a leak.
One night it seemed certain that she would sink.

"What a fool I was," Gilbert told his companions in grim humor, "ever to leave home at
all and come out here to feed the codfishes!" But
the leak was patched and the storms subsided.

There were other enemies to defeat besides bad
weather. The crew included some English deserters
and Boston convicts who had been forced to sail
on the American vessel. In mid-ocean they decided
to mutiny, take the ship to an English port and
receive the bounty which King George had offered
for American ships, and the reward that they would
surely get for Lafayette. One seaman divulged the

plot. Gilbert assembled the French officers and some trusted French and American sailors. With drawn swords they surrounded the ringleaders and clapped them in irons. That ended the threat of mutiny.

There was an amusing side to Lafayette's triumphant return to France. After all, he had left in defiance of the King's orders. Therefore, the King ordered his arrest and imprisonment. But the arrest was for only a week, the prison was his grandfather-in-law's luxurious palace. All was forgiven when Gilbert wrote a flowery letter of apology and regret to his monarch. How deeply his tongue must have been thrust in his cheek when he composed it!

His was a hero's welcome in the homeland from which he had secretly departed to fight for America. Now he was cheered in the streets, dined and wined and flattered in theaters. The lovely ladies of the court kissed him. The lovely Queen herself bestowed on him the rank of colonel and permitted him to buy—as was the custom then—the command of the King's Dragoons.

But more satisfactory than public acclaim was the happiness he found in his wife. Adrienne had grown greatly since his departure. Tragedy and grief had matured her. At nineteen she found that she could understand Gilbert, his reasons for leaving her and the greatness of his spirit. She stood by his side when Benjamin Franklin's grandson presented him with a gold-hilted sword, the token of America's appreciation. On the bow of the hilt was engraved "From the American Congress to Marquis de Lafayette, 1779."

Now Lafayette won France completely to the American cause. So many eager aristocrats and nobles wanted to fight for America. Some of them did. Amazingly influential, Lafayette wisely used his power to plead the cause of America with the French foreign ministry. He told the diplomats and military men that the United States could never win unless France sent vastly more aid, especially ships, money and supplies. He warned against the immediate dispatch of French troops because of American mistrust and jealousy of foreigners, now at fever pitch because of the bitter quarrels between some of the American generals and d'Estaing.

With Vergennes, the foreign minister, he discussed plan after plan: an invasion of Canada; an attack on Ireland; a joint French-Spanish expedition against England itself; and the levying of

Franklin's grandson presented a gold-hilted sword.

tribute on English coastal cities, the money to go to the American cause. Plan after plan was discarded. Only the dream of a great expedition to the aid of America persisted.

The American need for more help was urgent. Admiral d'Estaing had suffered a disastrous naval defeat at Savannah. Lafayette finally convinced the French leaders that France would have to enter the American conflict in full strength, if only to save her own forces already there. The fateful decision was made. More troops and ships would go to America.

The Marquis' cup of joy overflowed with the birth of a son on Christmas Eve, 1779. Joyfully Gilbert and Adrienne named the boy George Washington.

Preparing for the great expedition, Gilbert bought out of his own purse swords for his officers and uniforms for his men. He asked for command of the French forces which would go to America; but the war ministry was aware that older regular officers would resent his being placed over them. Instead, a veteran lieutenant general, the Count de Rochambeau, was selected to command the 6,000 men who would be sent in the fleet of Admiral de Ternay. All care was to be taken not to arouse more American resentment. The French troops were to be under Washington's orders; and American soldiers in all circumstances were to hold the honored right side of the line.

In the uniform of an American major general, Gilbert bade good-bye to his weeping Adrienne and to France; and, in the fast French frigate *Hermione,* he sped in advance of the slower expedition to tell Washington the great news.

Forty-eight days later the *Hermione* arrived in Boston port. The Marquis, who was not expected, was recognized by the crowds at the wharf; and the city turned out to greet him. Church bells rang in welcome. Guns roared salutes, and bonfires and fireworks blazed throughout the staid city. United States officials dined that night on the *Hermione*. Toasts were drunk to Washington and to France and a seventeen-gun salute roared out from the frigate's cannons.

Immediately Lafayette dispatched a joyful note to tell Washington of his arrival. After a two-week horseback journey, he met Washington at Morristown, New Jersey, just three days after the note arrived. Washington had wept with happiness when he read of Lafayette's return. He was happier still at Morristown when the Marquis told him of the coming of the French expedition. Lafayette had not dared to write this news from Boston for fear a letter might fall into British hands. Now he learned from his commander that the reinforcements were coming just in time. Not since the darkest days of Valley Forge had the plight of the Colonials been so bad.

The army was down to less than 6,000 all but

naked men, Washington said. These loyal die-
hards were short of pay and even shoes. For days
the hungry men lacked bread or meat. There was
no gold in the treasury, and the paper money had
become all but worthless. No wonder enlistments
had ceased!

Worse lay ahead. In May, Charleston would fall,
and Tarlton and Cornwallis would overrun the South.
In Camden, South Carolina, the Americans would be
disastrously defeated in July, losing more than a
thousand men captured and 900 killed, among
them the heroic de Kalb. Mutiny would haunt the
American ranks. One of the most trusted American
generals, Benedict Arnold, had turned traitor,
though Washington and America would not dis-
cover his treachery until the following September.
And a gallant young British officer, Major John
André, would be hanged as a spy for attempting
to pass through the American lines in civilian
clothes after meeting Arnold and getting valuable
information from him.

But now Washington and Lafayette talked joyfully together of the approach of the French fleet.
The General, who was having trouble with the
badly behaving Congress, asked the Marquis to

urge the government to take some decisive action now. Gilbert agreed to appear before Congress. Almost simultaneously with his appearance, the news leaked out that the French expedition was on its way. Once again the Americans, from Congress down to the hungriest soldier, were spurred to further resistance.

Feverishly, the Marquis and the others of Washington's loyal generals began putting the army into better shape so that the French would not be too downcast by what they found. A Canadian expedition was planned, and proclamations for the French Canadians were drawn up by Lafayette. These came into the hands of the traitor Benedict Arnold, who sent this information and much more to the British before he was found out.

On July 11th, Rochambeau and the French fleet arrived at Newport, Rhode Island. The French General turned out to be as curt and contemptuous to the Americans as Lafayette was warm and friendly. Rochambeau refused to deal with anyone but Washington. He disliked Lafayette and was jealous of him; but Gilbert served as a needed go-between, and Washington met and won over the crusty French general. Their joint conclusion was

that it was absolutely necessary for France to send
even more ships and men and funds to America.

But it would take a long time for the needed
reinforcements to arrive. Moreover, the grave
American situation was worsened by the treason
of General Arnold. He had been put in command
of the vital West Point fortress up the Hudson
River from New York, even though a court martial earlier in the year had found him guilty of
misusing funds in Philadelphia. This tragic man
who had been a hero of the unsuccessful invasion of Canada had become angry over real or
imagined mistreatment. He met British Major André
on the west bank of the Hudson, delivered to him
the plans of the fortress and revealed its weak
points so that it could be captured by the British.

On September 23rd André was captured by three
American militiamen. The plans were discovered
on him. But his captors did not know of Arnold's
part in the treachery and sent word to him of the
capture of André. Arnold immediately fled to a
British warship in the Hudson, and on the twenty-
ninth of September André was convicted as a
British spy.

The Marquis de Lafayette was a member of the

court martial of the gallant and popular young Englishman who had only done his duty as he saw it. For Gilbert it was the hardest task he had ever performed. The court martial ruled André must hang. In like manner the British had hanged as a spy a courageous American patriot named Nathan Hale, and Washington's generals could not forget.

After the court martial Gilbert walked weeping from the courtroom to Washington's headquarters. He begged him to commute the Major's sentence, or at least to permit him to die by musket fire, as a soldier, instead of by hanging. But Washington, listening to his other generals, stood firm. An example had to be made, they said. And so, on October 22nd, while Washington and Lafayette remained sadly in their quarters, Major André gave up his life for England.

Washington's and Rochambeau's assumption that the French force was not yet large enough was proved soon after the French fleet reached Newport. A vastly superior British fleet blockaded the port and bottled up the Frenchmen. Characteristically, the French officers set about enjoying themselves in town, much as had the British in Phila-

delphia and New York during the winter of
1777–78.

Gilbert chafed at the delay and lack of action.
Once again the Americans were despairing. Enmity
against the French was springing up. Congressional
factions fought among themselves. Discouraged,
the Marquis rejoined the Army in winter quarters
at New Windsor.

His fond hopes for an early American victory
through the aid of France were dead. His spirits
were low, not only because the country he had
adopted was in such danger, but also because the
bottling up of the French fleet was a blow to the
honor of France.

If possible, the new year of 1781 opened more
desperately for the Americans than had any other
year of the war. In January some veteran New
Jersey troops mutinied. The mutiny was put down
and two ringleaders were executed. The blockade
of the French fleet persisted. Rochambeau was
writing home that the situation was near hopeless.

Great Britain controlled the seas. Georgia, the
Carolinas and Virginia were under the thumb of
the British General Cornwallis. Clinton was firmly
based in New York.

No word had come of the requested French reinforcements. The Americans themselves seemed determined on self-destruction, for Congress wrangled and did little else. The New Englander, Samuel Adams, was seeking to arouse the people against Washington's conduct of the war. Washington himself wrote to Benjamin Franklin in faraway Versailles that if help did not come soon, the war for American independence would almost certainly be lost.

In these grim hours, Washington ordered Lafayette on a mission greatly to his and the commander's liking. The British had placed the traitor Arnold in command of the garrison at Hampton Roads, Virginia. Governor Thomas Jefferson of Virginia, the principal author of the Declaration of Independence, asked Washington for help against the British in his state. Washington proposed to Rochambeau that a joint French and American land and sea force be sent to capture the traitor.

With his division of light infantrymen, Lafayette set off to join forces with the French. He was impatient to capture Arnold and bring him back for the hanging he deserved.

But he and the French did not meet up. The French warships had delayed leaving Newport, and the British fleet had overtaken them at the entrance to Chesapeake Bay. After a brief action, the French were forced to seek the shelter of Newport again. Lafayette could not proceed against Arnold.

Then came an order from Washington which would affect the outcome of the war most decisively. Lafayette was instructed to join General Greene in the Carolinas, where major battles were being fought or were pending. The principal theater of the war had shifted southward.

Cornwallis, victorious in the Carolinas, was threatening Virginia from the south. Lord Clinton had also dispatched General Phillips to Virginia. This was the self-same Britisher who as an artillery officer in the Seven Years' War had commanded at Minden the artillery battery whose fire killed Lafayette's father. At all costs, ordered Washington, Lafayette must prevent the junction of Cornwallis and Phillips. Otherwise Virginia and the whole South could be lost.

By late April, Lafayette and his light infantrymen were in Alexandria, Virginia. Four days later General Phillips landed near Petersburg. The opposed forces raced for Richmond where many Continental supplies were stored. The Americans got there first, just in time to save the supplies.

The enraged Phillips died in a few days of a fever, and his command devolved on Benedict Arnold. To Washington's delight, Lafayette refused to treat with the traitor in a proposal for an exchange of prisoners. But the Marquis soon found himself in a dangerous position. Cornwallis had arrived at Petersburg and had joined forces with Arnold's men. Against less than a thousand Continentals, the British could array 7,500 troops. In a letter to de Noailles, his brother-in-law who was with the French forces in America, Lafayette said: "Your poor brother-in-law is devilishly busy getting himself licked."

And the jubilant Cornwallis wrote in an intercepted letter: "The boy cannot escape me!"

"The boy" did more than escape. In June, Lafayette was reinforced by Anthony Wayne's hard-bitten veterans. A week later he was joined by von Steuben. The war's climax was approaching. The juncture with Wayne, with Cornwallis in close pursuit, had been a brilliant maneuver. The unsuccessful Cornwallis, however, very nearly captured Governor Thomas Jefferson at Charlottesville.

Confidently, the Marquis decided to turn upon his pursuers. As Lafayette marched eastward to attack, Cornwallis for some mysterious reason fell back. Reinforced again by 600 mounted riflemen, Gilbert pressed the retreating British. Richmond was evacuated by Cornwallis on the twenty-first. The skirmishes were increasing. Cornwallis, despairing of conquering Virginia and confronted by the unexpectedly strong American force, began hurrying to Yorktown on the Virginia coast. There he planned to establish a base from which he could keep in sea communication with Clinton in New York and also be reinforced by water.

The unlucky Britisher and his tired troops arrived at Yorktown on August 1, 1781. It is a memorable date in our history; for Cornwallis' decision to hole up at Yorktown sealed his fate and led to the end of the war itself.

By a blessed coincidence, Washington had just gained fresh French reinforcements. Admiral de Grasse, commander of France's West Indian fleet, wrote that he would sail shortly from the West Indies with 3,000 French troops and all his men-of-war. He would be able to fight in America, he

said, until autumn, and would proceed to Yorktown. So Rochambeau, reluctant to attack New
York as Washington had planned, gladly joined his
French troops to Washington's army. Together they
struck out for Virginia.

In camp at Malvern Hill, Lafayette was impatient for action as usual. But it was imperative
for him to wait for reinforcements. De Grasse and
his men-of-war anchored off Yorktown on August
31st. There they set up a naval blockade of Cornwallis' garrison and landed troops the next day to
join Lafayette. Now Cornwallis was encircled by
land and sea. Early in September the French fleet
beat off attacking British vessels and Admiral de
Grasse sent ships up the Chesapeake Bay to bring
back Washington's and Rochambeau's combined
armies. Their goal was Williamsburg, Virginia, near
Yorktown.

The strange and unexpected end of the war was
fast approaching. The commander of de Grasse's
French troops, the veteran Marquis de Saint-Simon,
gallantly gave to General Lafayette the honor of
commanding his compatriots. The Frenchmen
urged now an immediate attack upon Cornwallis,
for the combined forces were strong enough. But

Gilbert declined because of his loyalty to Washington. He wanted his commander to have credit for the approaching triumph.

On September 14th, the historic juncture of the troops of Rochambeau and Washington, hastening down from Williamsburg, with the Americans and Frenchmen under Lafayette was effected below beleaguered Yorktown. Cornwallis gave up his outer fortifications on September 30th. The French and Americans brought up siege guns and began hammering at the British inner lines. Closer and closer drew the allies under the protective bombardment. Washington himself had fired the first cannon. Thomas Nelson, the new governor of Virginia who had just replaced Jefferson, aimed a cannon at his own home, which Cornwallis had made his headquarters. From the sea the French volleyed red-hot shot and shell into the town. But the British still held two strong redoubts from which they could pour murderous fire upon the entrenched Americans and French.

The joint commanders determined that these must be stormed. The honor of taking one was given to Lafayette, and to Baron de Vioménil of the French forces the second. Zero hour was set for eleven o'clock of the night of October 14th.

Under Lafayette and at the head of 400 selected light infantrymen were his faithful aide, Major Gimat, the noted young Alexander Hamilton and John Laurens, the son of the president of Congress. At eleven o'clock a signal rocket exploded above the attackers.

"Forward!" cried Lafayette.

In a cold rain the Americans and Frenchmen charged. Gimat was wounded. Hamilton, scrambling on his men's shoulders, stood on top of the parapet and leaped down among the enemy. Hand-to-hand fighting, bloody and brief, ensued. The first redoubt fell to the Americans under Lafayette in ten minutes. A few moments later the panting soldiers heard the shout of the French, "Vive le roi! Long live the king!" British resistance had almost ended.

Three days later Cornwallis sent an officer to the Americans. What would be the terms of victory? Washington said that only full surrender would be considered. At four o'clock in the afternoon the British gave in. And on October 19th, the 8,000 troops under Lord Cornwallis formally surrendered,

At eleven o'clock a signal rocket exploded above,

kilted Highlanders, blond German hirelings, red-coated Englishmen. Their flags were encased, and their bands played with wry humor an old British air, "The World Turned Upside Down." It certainly had.

The mortified Cornwallis himself was not present

and the Americans and Frenchmen surged forward.

for the final humiliation. He sent word that he was
ill. Perhaps he was. The surrender was taken for
Washington, at the commander's request, by General Benjamin Lincoln, whom Cornwallis had defeated at Charleston. In token of the surrender
General Lincoln received the sword of British

General O'Hara, instead of that of Cornwallis, as the happy but silent Americans looked on. Washington had ordered them not to cheer. He invited Cornwallis to dine with him that evening. The defeated, angry Britisher refused. Instead, he supped with the Frenchman, de Vioménil!

But no one really cared who ate with whom that night. Everyone knew that the victorious end of the Revolution was in sight. Britain wanted peace.

And no one, save Washington himself, could be given greater credit for the triumph of the brave little nation than the young French nobleman who loved it as his own.

5

GLORY AND A

DEEPENING SHADOW

An untried youth had sailed from France to America in the spring of 1777. The tested veteran of the American campaigns, who returned home to a hero's welcome in the winter of 1782, was even then only twenty-four years old. Yet in experience he was a mature man, skilled in warfare, wise in the ways of self-government, and determined that the reality of human freedom for which he had fought and which he had witnessed first-hand must not remain an unattainable dream for Frenchmen.

Had his king and his fellow nobles of France known of the democratic fire which burned in Gilbert's heart, he would not have been welcomed.

Instead, he would have been clapped into the dreaded political prison, the Bastille. There were imprisoned the enemies of the throne and any other unfortunates who had fallen out of favor. The belief that kings had a divine right to do as they pleased was dying hard. But it was dying even though the pleasure seekers at Versailles were not aware.

Lafayette came home to a deliriously Gallic welcome. His lovely wife had just received word of his arrival. As they met at the family palace, she fainted dramatically in his arms. The Parisian crowd screamed approval of their reunion. Some of his fellow nobles were envious of his glory. But almost all of France, from the favorites at court to the lowliest peasant, honored Lafayette as the darling of the nation.

The King questioned him closely about George Washington and what he stood for. Louis XVI did not know that this young Marquis supported ideas of man's rights far more radical than any held by America's revolutionary leaders.

Steadily Lafayette worked in the interests of the United States, taking part in the drawn-out peace negotiations and pleading successfully for money to help the infant country set itself straight. He had determined to journey briefly to America. But there was much to be done at the family home. Chavaniac needed his attention. The castle was in disrepair. The peasants faced crop failure, and food was scarce, even though the grain bins of the chateau itself were full. In the spring of 1783 his steward told him that since prices were high and food hard to find it was time to sell the grain.

"No," said the Marquis. "It is the moment to give it away." He ordered the grain distributed to the poor.

That was the voice of another kind of revolution.

In the hall of his newly purchased Paris home, he hung a copy of the Declaration of American Independence. Beside it was an empty space reserved for "the declaration of French rights."

With the signing of the Treaty of Versailles on September 3, 1783, the New and the Old World alike were at peace. The spirit of American freedom began to pervade Europe. Hopeful talk of liberty, equality and fraternity was heard both in aristocratic salon and in the meanly cobbled streets. But in the Palace of Versailles, Louis and

Marie Antoinette pursued their expensive pleasures. They seemed to believe that France's victory in America had brought happiness to their mistreated people. Little did they really know!

Meanwhile Lafayette longed to see the United States once more. Washington urged him to come as a guest of the nation. The young Frenchman in turn had much to report to his commander. So he sailed once again, on August 4, 1784. The roar of cannon, the shouting of the free men of America, all that he had come to like so well, again marked his arrival. For eleven days Lafayette visited Washington at Mount Vernon. There he told himself that he would someday become the Washington of France, for the spirit of free America, and the example of the greatest of Americans, inspired him as they always would.

At Mount Vernon Lafayette and Washington discussed slavery and its wrongs, the need for a strong central government, and the campaigns they had shared. Lafayette referred to himself as Washington's adopted son in every speech he made on his triumphal tour—in Baltimore, New York City, Albany, Hartford, Worcester, Boston, Richmond, Alexandria, Philadelphia, throughout Pennsylvania and at all the battlefields he had helped make immortal in American history. And just beyond the Alleghenies the state of Pennsylvania named a new county for him, the first of the hundreds of places throughout the nation that would someday bear his name.

At Annapolis he parted with Washington, the usually calm older man near tears, and the younger unashamed to weep. Never again would Gilbert see the patriot whom he worshiped as father and model, the leader who had molded him more than had any other person.

Early in 1785 Gilbert was back in France again. Almost immediately he resumed his effort to gain religious freedom for the French Protestants. Such freedom was a part of the American ideal.

He traveled throughout Europe, spreading revolutionary ideas. In Germany he met the great Prussian conqueror, Frederick the Great. As had other absolute and worried rulers of Europe, the Emperor asked him about democratic America.

Proud of his love for Washington and the United States and democracy, Gilbert spoke forthrightly.

"America will never have either royalty or nobility," he predicted.

This irritated the Emperor Frederick.

"Monsieur," he said, "I knew a young man who having visited countries where liberty and equality reigned, got it into his head to establish all that in his own country. Do you know what happened to him?"

At Annapolis Lafayette paid Washington a last farewell.

"No, sire," answered Lafayette.

"Monsieur," warned the Emperor, "he was hanged!"

At about this time, the French and Spanish planned to capture the English island of Jamaica in the West Indies. Admiral d'Estaing, who was to lead the expedition, asked Emperor Charles III of Spain to make Lafayette the chief of staff.

"No, no!" shouted the horrified monarch. "He would found a republic there!"

The Marquis' reputation was already frightening even kings.

The old Prussian Frederick and Charles III had enough sense to worry over what lay ahead in rebellious Europe. The Bourbons of France did not. Their ignorance spelled their doom, and it was nearer than anyone knew.

On the surface, life in France went on much the same. The hungry remained hungry, and the rich enjoyed themselves. In between, the small people, the middle classes of France, were sadly certain that death was in the air.

Constantly Gilbert corresponded with Washington. They exchanged gifts. Among them were fox-hounds and French pheasants from France to

Washington and to the Marquis, Virginia hams, ducks and mockingbirds.

Every American and every liberal Englishman who visited Paris became a guest of Lafayette. Thomas Jefferson, now the American envoy to France, was constantly in his home. And Gilbert, who might have built a bridge between the old way and the new, had royalty listened, was in equal favor at the court. There he urged reform, sought trade advantages for the United States, and told of the heady wonders of the free country of America, where liberty and equality reigned. He was the most persistent spokesman for freedom in the Old World.

But for the France which welcomed the American military victory, the American idea of the middle ground did not take deep enough root. France was too far gone, her rulers too removed from the people, her people too angry at the rulers for compromise. What suited freeborn Americans, the sons of independent Englishmen, was one thing. What the tormented, divided French must endure for eventual freedom was another, and a ghastly, course.

6

REVOLUTION

A victim of the French Revolution is reputed to have said, as she knelt beneath the guillotine's blade: "Oh, liberty, what crimes are committed in thy name!"

Whether or not these words were really uttered, they do speak for that terrible rebellion, so unlike our own. It is difficult for us to understand the inhuman days that marked the climax of the overthrow of absolute rule in France. We can have a glimmer of insight if we try to imagine the mistreatment of the common man, the peasant, the member of the middle class, the religious dissenter, even the protesting aristocrat in the days of French absolutism, and the animal-like existence of the mobs of Paris, the scum of city life.

In Bourbon France the life of a man counted for little more than the life of an alley cat. And in the city of Paris, the heart of France, the vengeful spirit of the mob boiled like a volcano. When men and women revolt after long mistreatment and persecution, there is not a clear-cut division between good and evil at first. Instead, a primary struggle rages, with the forces at one extreme and the forces at the other extreme determined to destroy all those who seek a middle ground.

This we have seen in our own day, in Hitler's Germany and in Communist Russia. France endured such a tragedy nearly 170 years ago. And the Marquis de Lafayette, a man of good will, lover of human freedom, the aristocrat who pitied the lowliest peasant, found himself squeezed and finally all but destroyed because he sought the middle road of democratic, constitutional government which he had learned first from his American friends.

The French Revolution began quietly enough. By 1787, the fat, pleasure-loving Louis XVI, warned by his ministers, had concluded that not even the American victories could satisfy his people. They were sick of royalty's excesses. They groaned under heavy taxes and were inflamed by the example of America and the preachings of their own scholars and philosophers who demanded an end to the right of kings to do as they pleased.

France was ripe for trouble. And the Marquis de Lafayette, newly returned from the victorious republic of the United States, was himself ready to lead the outraged people. Only, he wanted to do it in the constitutional way of America, the way which America had inherited from England, France's ancient enemy. He did not want to destroy. Instead, he wanted to build upon an orderly base as had the United States. Keep the king, he argued, but limit his powers with a constitution and an elected assembly.

Some of the King's advisers thought of calling together the States General, the ancient three-part assembly of the nation, which had not met since 1614. One part was composed of the nobility. The second part was composed of the clergy—the Roman Catholic hierarchy and priesthood which then exercised a tremendous influence in government in France. At the tail end was the third estate, the middle-class and common people of France without noble or religious title.

But such a gathering might be too radical. Instead it was determined to call together the Assembly of Notables, a gathering of the nobility and other established leaders of the nation. Let the Notables pass upon France's troubles, the King's spokesmen decided.

The Marquis de Lafayette had been placed on the Notables list, then removed because the regime was afraid of his wild ideas, and finally put back again. He punned that the Assembly of Notables was an assembly of the "not-ables," a proof that he could joke in two languages.

The King opened the meeting of the Assembly of Notables at Versailles on the morning of February 21, 1787. Before it ended, Lafayette became for a while France's most popular figure. But to the King and Queen and their court, he became the most dangerous man in the nation.

The Notables were to discuss principally tax reform and to make recommendations for strengthening the finances of France. But the Marquis had other ideas. Abruptly he demanded a reduction of royal spending and an end to corruption and abuses by the court's favorites. The money they squandered, he told the King in a bold statement, had been taken out of the sweat and tears and blood of the people.

The King thought of having him thrown into the Bastille. But Lafayette was too well liked. And next Lafayette proposed a National Assembly, going beyond the idea of a meeting of the States General. The King was asked also to permit assemblies in all the provinces of France, to allow changes in the harsh laws of punishment for offenders, and to give full civil rights to the Protestants.

Provincial assemblies were formed. It was not too good an idea, from the King's point of view, because several of these refused to approve tax raises. Members of the nobility in the provinces, no less than the oppressed middle classes and poor, were growing more and more angry at the heavy taxation. As indignation rose, four groups plotted for power. The first of these were the King's own allies. They wanted nothing changed and were furious at the spirit of revolt among the people.

Another, led by the Duke d' Orleans, a brother of the King, conspired to overthrow the monarch and assume power for the Duke. The Duke had some democratic ideas, but there was no honesty in him. He was a ruthless, immoral, selfish man, ready to destroy anyone who stood in his way. But because he pretended to side with the people, he was popular with them.

A third group was made up of the truly murderous revolutionaries who wanted to destroy everything that smacked of royalty, pluck two eyes for one and set up a dictatorship of their own.

Against these stood Lafayette and others who wanted a constitutional monarchy. They proposed a nation headed by a king, but with the real powers of government vested in elected parties, with a constitution or an established statement of rights. Lafayette and his associates hoped to make France democratic in the English and American tradition. They wanted to do it in the most legal and peaceful way possible.

There were other schemers, many of them in the pay of more than one side. One such was a brilliant, wicked plotter, the Count de Mirabeau. Like the Duke d' Orleans, he would seek Lafayette's destruction. And there were the Parisian mobs, ignorant, cruel and easily misled, ready to rise and destroy, prey to the plotters who sought to arouse them for their own wicked purposes.

Nowhere have there ever assembled more repulsive and terrifying bands than the mobs of Paris. They were largely made up of thieves and murderers and harlots, deserters from the army, diseased and hopeless derelicts. They were despairing, hungry and hopeless men and women, little more than beasts who in their blind rage were ready to tear down and destroy anyone or anything. It was the mob, led by a passion for destruction, which would bathe Paris in blood.

The King, at his wits' end, was now willing to do anything to try to avoid revolution. So he convened the States General.

The ragged, scowling people of Paris did not cheer the nobles or the clergy when at last those two groups and the representatives of the ordinary people paraded in colorful pomp from church to the great meeting hall in Versailles. Only the commoners were cheered by the populace. That should have been a warning of bloody events to come.

When the sessions began, the commoners finally won what Lafayette had sought, a true National Assembly. And after the Assembly convened, the

Marquis electrified the nation on July 11, 1789, with a stirring document. This was his own declaration of the rights of man, based upon the American Declaration of Independence and upon the liberal ideas of the philosophers of France.

By then the Parisians were getting out of hand. Street fights raged, and the mob even skirmished with the King's palace troops, the Swiss Guards. The National Assembly voted to remain in permanent session, hoping that its sought-for reforms could bring peace.

But the people had tasted the fruit of liberty. On July 14th the Assembly debated Lafayette's declaration of rights. At the same time the mob stormed the hated Bastille, massacring its defenders and setting loose its prisoners. This mass assault was to be remembered as marking France's dawn of liberty. The King, hearing that there was trouble in the city, asked if a riot was in progress.

"No, sire, not a riot," answered one of his courtiers. "It is a revolution."

The disturbed King came to the National Assembly, appealing for help. An emergency force was created by the Assembly. It was to be known as the National Guard and to be formed of volunteer

Parisian citizens of all classes. Lafayette was named commanding general. At first the National Guard was a motley group, without uniforms and in some cases without arms, except for homemade weapons. But these citizen-soldiers did try bravely to preserve order.

By now the Paris mob was running amuck, butchering and beheading its victims and parading around with their heads on pikes. Only Lafayette seemed to have any influence over these madmen. Single-handed, he snatched prisoners away from the mob. Everywhere he went, the rioters, even the most murderous, would listen to him and cheer him.

Soon after the fall of the Bastille, he ordered that the Bastille itself—that symbol of royal oppression—be destroyed. This was revolutionary France's day of days.

But the mobs got out of hand again and again, driven by fear of starvation, by hate, and by the prodding of rumor-spreading agents of political rivals and revolutionists who wanted to destroy the rule of the royal Bourbon family.

The crimes committed by the mobs were so barbarous as to be beyond belief. Only the National Guard under Lafayette saved Paris and France. Probably Lafayette could have become dictator of France, the ruler of what was then the second most powerful nation in the world. But he did not seek such power. Instead he dreamed of a real democracy for France.

In October, for two dreadful days, not even Lafayette and his National Guardsmen could hold the mob in check. It is probable the people were stirred up by agents of the Duke d' Orleans. This ambitious brother of the King urged them to march on Versailles where Louis XVI was virtually a prisoner.

All the while hunger stalked Paris and France. Unemployment was rising because of the flight of so many wealthy royalists. On October 5th, the story spread that some lower-class Parisian housewives had been told by the bakers that there was no bread.

Whether this was the truth or a planted rumor, the gutter folk of Paris went wild. They cursed Lafayette himself, pelted the members of the National Guard with bricks, and broke into the Hôtel de Ville, center of government for the city of Paris, looting and pillaging.

When they heard the rumor "No bread," the gutter folk of Paris went wild.

Lafayette summoned his guardsmen. But the mob was completely out of hand. Armed with pistols, pikes, knives, pitchforks and guns, they hemmed in the guardsmen themselves.

"On to Versailles!" they yelled. Some even shouted that Lafayette must be hanged.

The Marquis walked out among them, as if daring them to touch him. Pistols were leveled at him and then turned aside. Agitators shouted for a march on Versailles, where dwelt the King and Queen.

Lafayette determined to withstand them. This was not orderly revolution as he had seen it in America. This was anarchy.

He rushed to the National Assembly. The mob had invaded the seat of government, screaming insults in the seats of the deputies. Ironically, it had violated the Assembly on the very day that its president had obtained the King's signature to the still incomplete new constitution and the declaration of the rights of man. As the president read the King's approval, the mob cried, "Will that give bread to the poor?"

Next Lafayette rode to Versailles. For the time being the rioters did not try to enter the residence of the King. But there was hatred in the eyes of the courtiers when Lafayette entered, even though he was there to protect their monarch.

The King asked him what the people wanted. He answered, "Bread."

Through the night Lafayette remained awake and on guard. Then he returned to Paris exhausted. In the early morning he was summoned again. The mob had broken loose at the King's chateau. Before Lafayette reached Versailles, the mob had slaughtered many of the bodyguard and even invaded the Queen's bedroom. She had escaped through a secret passage to the King's own chambers. Inside and outside the chateau, the people were shouting their hatred of the Queen and demanding that the King come to Paris.

On sudden inspiration, Lafayette went to the Queen who was cowering in the King's chambers with her children. He persuaded her to come with him out on the balcony in plain view of those who were crying for her life. There he took off his hat, bowed, dropped to his knees and kissed her hands. In a sudden about-face, the fickle Parisians began screaming, "Long live the Queen! Long live Lafayette!"

Then, drawing to him a member of the King's Guard, Lafayette took the blue, white and red cockade of the Revolution from his own hat, thrust it into the guardsman's hat, and threw his arms about him. The crowd then cheered the lucky soldier whose brothers-in-arms they had so recently been butchering. Such is the way of mobs.

But the Parisians had their way. The King agreed to go to Paris, protected by the National Guard and accompanied by Lafayette.

At length the procession reached the city. It was flanked by the wildly shouting people. Lafayette escorted the royal family, now virtual prisoners of the Parisians, to the palace of the Tuileries.

These had been a terrible two days for France. Lafayette was sure that the rioting had been the work of agents of the Duke d' Orleans. Therefore he sought out the Duke and told him that he had to leave the country.

"The King has descended several steps of his throne," the Marquis said. "But I have placed myself on the last. He will descend no further and in order to reach him you will have to pass over my body."

Four days later the Duke left for London.

Now throughout France lawlessness prevailed. Royalists were fleeing from certain death. Each day Lafayette and his National Guard quelled riots and disorders. A plot to assassinate him failed, but his life was constantly in danger. And matters went from bad to worse throughout the fall and winter and spring.

Even so, on July 14, 1790, France celebrated the fall of the Bastille in magnificent fashion. Nearly 200,000 people gathered on the Champs de Mars outside Paris for the spectacle. The King and Queen themselves were seated in state before them. The volatile French feasted and danced and applauded as the National Guard and detachments of the regular army and navy paraded across the plain. Now in persistent contradiction they shouted their approval of Lafayette as he rode at the head of his troops. That day two hundred priests celebrated a solemn mass on the Champs de Mars; and as the mass ended, Lafayette drew his sword and waved it over his head.

At that signal the National Assembly repeated the oath of constitutional brotherhood. Again Lafayette's sword waved. The King, now called "King of the French" instead of "King of France" repeated an oath to maintain the constitution which was being produced by the National Assembly.

The crowd cheered everybody: Lafayette, the King, the Queen and their little son, whom the Queen held before the people. And in the dramatic kind of ceremony which the French loved so well, Lafayette galloped up to the great national altar. Dismounting he walked slowly up a flight of stairs, bowed before the altar, laid his sword upon it, and swore to be faithful to country, the law and the King, and to uphold the constitution of France. Behind him the assembled thousands shouted together, "We swear."

From this day of unity there might have come a peaceable acceptance of constitutional law. But this was not to be. Miserable France, rebelling against the misrule of Louis XVI and his forebears, was not the America of Jefferson, Adams, Franklin, Washington and the sons of Englishmen long used to some freedom. Mistreatment had gone too far and lasted too long.

7

A NATION IN RUINS

The outward coming together of Frenchmen at the celebration of the fall of the Bastille and at the formal acceptance of the constitution was short-lived. Seemingly the nation was bent on destroying herself, even without the assistance of the surrounding enemies who were determined to restore the Bourbon King to power.

How France survived as a nation remains almost a miracle. And it is nearly as hard to understand how Lafayette himself lived through those frightful days and months and years. Although protector of the King, Lafayette had rebelled against him. So he was hated by the royal family whom he safeguarded. He was no less opposed by those radical

French leaders who had no use for his dreams of a constitutional monarchy. These zealots wanted to destroy the royal family and any vestige of kingly rule, and place all power in themselves for the exercise of their extreme ideas.

The worst and most successful of Lafayette's revolutionary enemies formed a club named the Jacobins. Eventually the Jacobins inspired the Reign of Terror in which many hundreds of French men, women and even children were to die senselessly beneath the guillotine.

Plots against Lafayette's life were continuous. He lost favor among the fickle populace after a revolt of some French soldiers in the city of Nancy. They were under the command of one of his cousins, and he ordered the commander to take all necessary means to put down the rebellion. The stern and bloody repression of the revolt was blamed on Lafayette.

The Paris mob, protesting "the massacre of Nancy" and incited by his enemies was turned back by Lafayette at the head of his Guardsmen. Again he was hated. And his enemies took advantage of his new unpopularity. They made him the victim of libels and rumors, widely circulated by mouth and in printed pamphlet. The Jacobins openly demanded that Lafayette be executed. But he clung to his hope for a peaceable and lawful France under a constitutional monarchy. He had no ambition, he told his questioners, other than the public good.

Mirabeau, president of the Jacobins, died in April, 1791, but that did not mean an end to factionalism and strife.

The Easter of 1791 brought Lafayette to the breaking point. The King had decided to attend Easter services at a church in the suburb of St. Cloud. The mob, always ready for trouble, heard of the King's plan and determined to prevent his attendance and thus humiliate him. Egged on by Jacobin leaders, an unruly crowd hemmed in the King's coach so that it could not proceed.

Lafayette made his way to the coach and shouted to his Guardsmen to disperse the gathering. But the Guard had been penetrated by agents of the Jacobins and of the Duke d' Orleans. The troops refused to move against the shouting horde. Lafayette summoned a loyal battalion known as the Carmelites. But as they prepared to attack the mob, the King and Queen slipped back into the palace in defeat.

Lafayette urged poor Louis to come out and go to St. Cloud. Otherwise he knew the mob would register a victory against law in the person of the King. But the frightened ruler-in-name-only refused.

In disgust, Lafayette wrote out his resignation as commander of the National Guard. It had disobeyed his orders. At the Hôtel de Ville, he presented the resignation to the Commune—the revolutionary governing body of Paris. He told his reasons and fainted in anger. The next day, ashamed representatives of the National Guard pledged to obey him and the law. They presented this pledge to him and dramatically begged him to return to command. Lafayette could not resist. For a while there was real order in Paris.

And then the King himself brought on a crisis that helped only his enemies. He and the Queen, prompted by some of their courtiers, decided to go back on their pledge and flee France. If they could cross the border, perhaps many Royalist Frenchmen would join them and the monarchs of

Austria and Prussia in an invasion of France that
would restore the King to his throne.

Louis and Marie Antoinette fled by coach during the night of June 20th. Their flight was not
discovered until the next morning.

Lafayette was awakened with the surprising and
dangerous news that the royal family was missing.
That morning new cries of denunciation rose against
him as enemy agents quickly spread word that he
had conspired with the King.

"Traitor! Traitor!" shouted the mob.

Never before had Lafayette been called that
worst of epithets. But disdainful and unafraid, he
signed an order for the arrest of the King. No
Frenchman had ever before given a command for
the arrest of his sovereign.

In the turmoil, the mob invaded the Tuileries
only to be driven out at Lafayette's order. The
people feared now a counter-revolution by the
King's sympathizers. So did the Assembly, which
declared itself in permanent session. That day, at
a meeting of the Jacobins, Lafayette was subject
to torrents of abuse. And then the King's where-
abouts was learned. He had been arrested at
Varennes.

In a short while the royal fugitives returned in their captive coach, discouraged, tired, sullen and unrepentant. The mob, surging about the palace, sought not the lives of the fugitives, but those of the three bodyguards they had taken with them. The unfortunate men were seized and would have

During the night the King and Queen fled by coach.

been torn apart had not Lafayette and his men rescued them.

Now the King was indeed a prisoner. His life, although he did not know it, was already forfeit.

The Assembly rushed now to complete the troublesome constitution, which had been approved long before it had been fully drawn up. Once again the radicals plotted to invade the Assembly and the Tuileries.

In a bloody riot on the Champs de Mars, soon after the second anniversary of the fall of the Bastille, troops under Lafayette's orders fired upon the rioters, killing many of them. Again he was reviled. But the Assembly, in spite of everything, finished the constitution. It was accepted in all particulars by the King. What else could he have done?

In September another great celebration was held at the Champs de Mars. And for the second time Lafayette rode at the head of his National Guard of citizen soldiers to the nation's altar.

On the last day of September Louis XVI declared the session of the Assembly ended. As the King closed the Assembly, the president said to him, "Sire, in accepting the constitution, you have ended the revolution."

But the revolution of blood was only beginning.

Lafayette presented his resignation, bade farewell to the National Guard and, bearing with him a sword made from the locks of the Bastille and presented to him by the Assembly, he set out for Chavaniac. No longer was he a marquis. The Assembly had voted to do away with all titles of nobility. He was now plain Citizen-General Lafayette.

So, after fourteen years of war and revolution he turned to the ways of peace. The old chateau was handsomely redecorated. Lafayette, surrounded by his wife and family, was content; or, if not content, he was at least ready for a rest.

But he was not destined for a life of peace. In the royal palace, the Queen herself became active in politics. Unaware that men she was aiding would someday take her life, she supported the candidacy of a notorious Jacobin, Petion, for mayor of Paris. The rabble wanted him too, and he was elected. With his victory, the friends of orderly government, the Fayettists, lost control in Paris. The revolution would be bloody business now.

One December day, a courier arrived at Chavaniac from Paris. France was on the brink of war. The King, at the urging—and virtual order—of the minister of war, had summoned Lafayette to command one of the three armies which would defend France.

What had happened was inevitable. Thousands of royalist officers of the French Army, loyal to the King and mostly centered at Coblentz just across the Rhine, had threatened to invade France.

Even though these men were loyal to him, the prisoner-king, Louis XVI, was forced to notify the German and Austrian rulers that if the armed French refugees would not disperse war would be declared. The refugees continued to prepare for battle.

Lafayette hastened to Paris. Once more he was a national hero. Soon he was in the frontier city of Metz, where long ago he had first heard of the American war for freedom. He had little respect for the army he would now help command. The men were badly trained, clothed and armed. Jacobin agents had been inciting them. At least a third of their officers had deserted because of their royalist sympathies and were even now planning with their fellow fugitives the invasion of France. Two other generals shared command.

Resolutely Lafayette set about to make an army out of the discontented men. He gained time when the Germans agreed to scatter the royalists. But all knew that this was only a postponement of certain war. The minister of war, Narbonne, held council with the three generals. Lafayette would invade the Low Countries. Rochambeau, his old comrade in America, would remain in support of him. The third general, Lückner, would maneuver at the Rhine River to keep the enemy guessing.

But Lafayette's enemies were scheming against the minister of war. He was ousted, and the radicals took over. Soon the Jacobins demanded Lafayette's head because of his political activity against them. They were led by some of the most bloodthirsty fanatics of all time—Robespierre, Danton and Marat, whose names would soon be whispered in horror in all of France.

The new Jacobin minister of war, Dumouriez, changed the plans for the campaign. Later he would turn traitor to France. Accepting the new orders, Lafayette moved against the enemy; and before April was out, he was fighting the Austrians. But he made war with sinking spirits because of what he heard from Paris. The Jacobins were in almost full control. Law and order were giving way to dictatorial rule. Hoodlums and terrorists roamed the Paris streets at will in behalf of the radicals.

Raging with anger, Lafayette wrote a fiery letter to the Assembly, denouncing the Jacobins. It was read in the Assembly amid loud disorder. That

The mob broke into the palace and insulted the King.

night the Parisian Jacobins charged that Lafayette was in league with the monarchs of Europe to conquer France. The Jacobin clubs throughout the nation joined in the denunciation.

On June 20th, a mob broke into the Tuileries,

opened up the cellars and guzzled before the King and Queen and blew tobacco smoke in their faces. They even made the King himself put on the red cap of the revolution and drink with their drunken leaders.

Hearing of the outrage, Lafayette determined to return to Paris. General Lückner warned that his enemies would cut off his head. But back he went, accompanied only by an aide and his valet. Striding into the Assembly on June 28th, Lafayette urged the members to punish the invaders of the Tuileries and to destroy the Jacobin clubs. But the Assembly itself was now almost entirely under the domination of the Jacobins. It would do nothing. Out to the Tuileries he went. The King was almost friendly now, for here at least was someone whom he could trust even though the two men had so long been ranged against each other. But the Queen was still contemptuous and aloof.

"Better perish utterly than be saved by Lafayette," she said. She spoke more truly than she knew.

Lafayette gathered together some officers of the National Guard of proven integrity and pleaded with them to hold against the radicals. They promised to do so. Now he had to return to the army. Once again he wrote a letter of denunciation to the Assembly though he must have known that there was not much he could do to resist the Jacobins.

In desperation he decided to take the King away from Paris, else constitutional government would die. He planned for the King to declare full support of the constitution under Lafayette's military protection. Together they would lead the soldiers of France to Paris and overthrow the Jacobins. The constitutional monarchy would become a reality.

But when the King was told of the plan, he and his advisers rejected it. They were too hopeful that the Prussian and Austrian armies and the royalist refugee officers would score a great victory. Then the old days would return.

Said Marie Antoinette to Lafayette's emissaries: "We are very grateful to your general, but it would be better for us to be shut up for two months in a tower."

Then the pompous Prussians and Austrians issued a statement to the French nation which united the people against the common outside foe and thereby placed France in the hands of the Jacobins. The Prussian and Austrian rulers declared haughtily that if the Tuileries were invaded again or any attack made on the royal family, Paris would be "given up to military execution and the guilty rebels to the death they have deserved."

Patriotic Frenchmen, forgetting political differences, and even their dread of the Jacobin leaders, rushed to enlist in the army. They marched to a stirring new song, written by a patriotic composer, Rouget de Lisle. It would be known as "The Marseillaise" and would become the anthem of France.

The story got out that Lafayette had plotted to march on Paris. His enemies sought to have him branded a traitor by the Assembly. But Lafayette was so revered that the Assembly refused by a vote of nearly two to one, despite Jacobin threats.

Again the mobs were called into play by the debased Jacobins. On August 10th, the berserk underworld once again invaded the Tuileries. This time its savagery raged unchecked. There was no Lafayette near. The King's brave Swiss Guards were massacred almost to a man and their heads carried aloft on pikes. They had not even resisted the invaders, for the King had foolishly ordered them not to, and they died under the butcher knives and clubs and pikes of the inhuman rabble.

Never before had France witnessed such a day. The Jacobins had imprisoned the King and his royal family. The evil Danton had been named minister of justice. There would be no justice now. The Assembly had fled. The constitution had no meaning. Liberty had perished. France, attacked from without, writhed under the heel of the Jacobin fanatics.

But even now Lafayette did not give up. He was sure that if he raised the standard of liberty the people would come to the support of the constitution and King. Under the protection of his army the Assembly could meet elsewhere than Paris. He was confident that his troops would remain loyal to him and to the constitution. But when he drew them up in battle array at Sedan, many refused to take the oath to support the constitution. The Jacobins had kept busy. And the Jacobin leaders had an incredible offer to make to him. If he would abandon King and constitution, they would make him president of the republic they planned.

Of course he refused, but he was almost alone. Other generals of the armies were giving in to the new rulers of France. And on the seventeenth, the Jacobins' executive council ordered Lafayette to turn over his command to their man, Dumouriez, and to return immediately to Paris. This meant but one thing. He would be accused of treason and would be beheaded.

Lafayette conferred with two close friends and comrades-in-arms, La Tour-Maubourg and Bureaux de Pusy. If they wanted to live, they decided, they must flee. Someday they could again serve their nation.

So, on Sunday morning, August 19th, a little group of seventeen officers and twenty-four servants and orderlies, set out on horseback toward the French frontier. They planned to make their way to Holland and thence to America. Faithful to the last, Lafayette had drawn up all plans necessary for the security of his army and the border they guarded. To his general officers he left orders as to what they should do if the Prussians and Austrians should attack.

Even as they crossed the border and entered what is now Belgium, the Jacobin assembly was approving a decree that branded him a rebel and conspirator against liberty. The command went out throughout all France to arrest him.

In this hour of despair with death waiting for him in his homeland, Lafayette and his followers were captured in the Belgian town of Rochefort as they sought lodging. Under a heavy guard of Austrian hussars they were taken to Namur, the enemy headquarters.

8

TRIUMPH OVER TRAGEDY

Now came years of torment for the captive Lafayette and for the French nation which lay almost in ruins.

There was no forgiveness or mercy in the hearts of the Austrians and Prussians toward these lost leaders of the Revolution, the noble enemies of royalty, who had fallen into their hands as they crossed the border. Lafayette and his comrades—La Tour-Maubourg, Bureaux de Pusy, and Lameth, a one-time political enemy who had joined them in flight—were separated from their less feared companions. The common soldiers and officers of the line, men with no political background, were ordered out of the country. A second group, made up of those who had not been leaders or policy makers in revolutionary France, were imprisoned in Antwerp. They did not suffer greatly.

But iron-handed mistreatment was to be the lot of Lafayette for five dreadful years. He was mocked in the streets of Luxembourg on his way to his first prison at Wesel. There he and his associates were lodged in dark, separate dungeons. They could not see each other, write letters or be given any news of the world. No exercise was permitted. Every minute of day and night they were

Rats swarmed through the filthy prison cells.

watched by guards. Rats swarmed through their cells, and the hated prisoners suffered fever and cold so that Lafayette came near dying. Such was to be their treatment almost throughout their captivity.

Once Lafayette was offered a chance for an easier life. The brutal king of Prussia wrote that he would be better treated if he would give information which Austria and Prussia could use against France. Indignantly, Lafayette refused.

As the year ended, the imprisoned Frenchmen were transferred to the fortress of Magdeburg. Their captors sought to misuse them by making them travel in the cold open air; but fresh, clean air was precisely what the pent-up men needed. Their health improved temporarily. At Magdeburg things were a little better, at least as concerned news of the outside world. For here it was possible to smuggle out letters now and then, and receive them through the aid of friendly, bribe-minded guards.

It is just as well that Lafayette did not know much of what was happening in France. His dear wife, almost out of her mind with anxiety, had not learned until August 24th whether he was dead or alive. She had hidden his secret papers, buried his swords and other awards, sent young George to hiding in the mountains, and was making ready to flee with her family to England, as Lafayette had advised her, when she was arrested.

The brave Adrienne demanded permission to remain at Chavaniac on parole. Somehow, the request was granted. There she sought to help her husband. She wrote to President Washington, imploring his aid. But the head of a young republic had to act carefully in European matters. Washington did send money for her use and tried quietly to do more through agents in Europe. Gouverneur Morris, the American minister and an old friend, placed 100,000 livres at her disposal. But by the spring of 1793, Adrienne had given up hope.

France itself was mercilessly drowning in her own blood. Monstrous, cruel men, fighting for power among themselves and for the absolute destruction of all vestiges of the old France, had turned the nation into a vast execution chamber. Throughout the provinces raged bloody civil war, as Royalists and plain folk, aroused by the Terror in Paris, warred against the Republican forces. In Paris the savagery of the Jacobins, the outrageous excesses of the mob and the brutality of criminals conspired to create a hideous nightmare of murder.

In September, new Jacobin decrees did away with what human rights remained in France. More terrible persecutions began. To be suspect meant that the suspected person could be sent to the guillotine for no proved cause, and thousands died. The King was guillotined, and after him the Queen and the little Dauphin. The Reign of Terror raged everywhere.

Finally, on November 12th, Adrienne herself was summoned before a revolutionary commission and sent to prison without trial. There she labored to ease the lives of the doomed women about her while waiting for the death she believed was certain. In prison also were her mother and grandmother and her devoted sister, Louise.

Of all this Lafayette was ignorant. On January 4, 1794, he was transferred to still another prison, at Neisse on the Polish frontier. This journey in freezing weather was also of great benefit to his health. There, in his lonely dungeon beneath the ramparts of the fort, he was permitted a few more privileges.

But he did not remain long at Neisse. Soon he

was transferred to the grim prison at Olmutz, the ancient capital of Moravia, one of the petty German states, whose humble immigrants to Pennsylvania had treated his wound in 1777.

With him went La Tour-Maubourg and de Pusy, and their servants. They were still jailed apart. And at Olmutz they were robbed of the little that remained to them—watches and knee buckles, collar buckles, even razors. All books in which the word "liberty" could be found were taken away.

The Prussian jailers were more brutal than any the prisoners had known. Lafayette could not see beyond the walls of his cell. He was not permitted to write or receive letters, and bribery was nearly impossible here. Their guards and jailers would not even speak their names. The prisoners were simply numbers. They were allowed neither knives nor forks, for their jailers pretended to fear that they might commit suicide with them.

But Lafayette's courage lived on. To his captors he said proudly, "Messieurs, I am not obliging enough to kill myself!"

A lesser man most certainly would have tried to do away with himself. Close by the fortress threaded the rank open sewers of the town. Mosquitoes swarmed upon the imprisoned men. The air was almost always thick with fog. A guard of thirty troops watched them constantly. Their doors were opened only for meals. Their clothes hung in rags. They drank dirty water from pots which were left in the corridor beyond their cell doors.

Then in November, 1794, an unexpected and gallant attempt was made to free Lafayette. The prison physician, a friendly enough man named Haberlein, admired Washington. When no one was around, he talked sometimes with Lafayette about the American Revolution. One day he told the General that he had met in the town of Olmutz a friend of Lafayette named Dr. Bollman.

Never had Lafayette heard of anyone of that name. Instantly he reasoned that some plot was being hatched in his behalf. He got word to his companions that plans to escape might be in the making. Through the agreeable and possibly ignorant physician, he and the mysterious Bollman began exchanging notes written in lemon juice so that they could be read only when held against fire.

A daring plan was agreed upon. Lafayette was to persuade his jailers to permit him to take a carriage drive now and then for his health. This he was soon permitted, under guard. Bollman, whoever he was, and whatever friends he had with him, would be on the alert. They would recognize him when he rubbed his brow with a handkerchief. As for the rest, that would be up to the conspirators, to Lafayette's own courage and to fate.

The Marquis would not know for a long time who Justus Erich Bollman was. But to this twenty-five-year-old German student, Lafayette had long been an idol. He had become intimately acquainted with refugee friends of Lafayette in England and with them had plotted the General's escape. Bravely the young German had agreed to be the instrument of deliverance.

As a German subject of the king of England, Bollman was entitled to go to Germany. There, after much intelligent questioning, he decided that Lafayette must be at Olmutz. And in a coffee house in Vienna, after a first trip to Olmutz, he met a twenty-one-year-old American student, Francis Kinloch Huger of Charleston, South Carolina. This was the boy who as a small child in 1777 had watched his father greet the young Marquis de Lafayette when the *Victoire* anchored off the South Carolina coast. Gladly the daring American joined the conspiracy. With Huger posing as a young English gentleman and Bollman as his tutor, they set out with extra saddle horses and a coach filled with luggage, hidden rope ladders and other equipment for the escape.

In November Dr. Haberlein told Lafayette that his friend Bollman was leaving on the eighth. That was the signal. The eighth was the day for his carriage drive—the day for the attempt at escape!

Out of the prison on that Saturday, October 8th, lurched the little carriage bearing Lafayette, with a corporal near him and another soldier beside the driver.

Soon Lafayette suggested a drink for the guard. The carriage drew up at a little inn.

In the distance the General saw two horsemen. As they passed the coach, he wiped his forehead. Then he asked permission to take a walk in company with the corporal.

Together he and the corporal strolled along the road. Behind them the two horsemen had turned and were riding toward them. Pretending that he wanted to examine the corporal's sword, Lafayette put his hand on it.

But the corporal, alarmed by the sound of hoof-beats, snatched away the sword. He and Lafayette struggled violently. Lafayette pushed his hand into the corporal's mouth to still his cries, and the corporal bit him so hard that his hand bled. By then Huger and Bollman had reached him. Atop the coach the driver sat trembling with fright. The other guard was running toward the town, screaming for help.

Huger handed Lafayette a pair of pistols, thrust a bridle into his hands and shouted something which Lafayette thought was "Go off."

But what he actually said was "Go to Hoff," a little village where carriages, servants and other conspirators waited. The misunderstanding, and nothing else, meant failure. Away Lafayette galloped in his prison rags, his back badly sprained from his tussle with the corporal, and his hand bleeding. The brave youngsters, Bollman and Huger, tried to ride away on the single remaining horse. The steed, refusing to carry both, threw them, and Huger insisted that Bollman remount. Away sped the German as the young American gave himself up to the swarming guards of Olmutz. Later Bollman was captured.

Lafayette fled as Huger fell from the other horse.

And Lafayette, too, was seized after a mad ride of eight leagues to the little town of Sternberg. There a peasant betrayed the prisoner who had always been the friend of the peasants and the poor. He almost talked his way out of his predicament by persuading the magistrate before whom he was brought that he was a merchant who had lost his way.

Then someone in the crowd called out: "He looks like General Lafayette." The magistrate said to him that they must wait until word came from Olmutz.

"I am Lafayette," the prisoner said proudly. The game was up. The prisoner was taken back to Olmutz and to worse treatment.

Bollman and Huger were lucky. They were kept imprisoned in irons, true enough, and their trial lasted for eight weeks. But it ended in a surprisingly light prison sentence of six months. They served their time, and got over the border. This was just before the arrival of an order from the Austrian emperor that their case should be reopened—no doubt with a more severe sentence in mind.

Despairing at last, his wounded hand troubling him and his spine wracked with pain, Lafayette lay alone again in the dark cell at Olmutz.

Back in Paris the Reign of Terror was reaching its climax of human butchery. Robespierre, the arch-revolutionist, was sending to the guillotine anyone who disagreed with him. Among them were his old comrades Danton and Desmoulins, who had doomed many another. Sixty a day, the heads rolled—heads of aristocrats and nobles, of lesser men and women whose only crime was their decency, of political schemers and terrorists, soldiers who had failed in battle—whoever Robespierre thought stood in the way of himself and of the France he was determined to rule. The Duke d' Orleans, the Bourbon who had plotted against his kinsman and king, died too, a victim of the excesses which he had in part brought about.

Fortunately, Lafayette's wife survived the terror, probably because of American efforts in her behalf. But her mother and grandmother and sister Louise were executed before the reaction against Robespierre set in. Soon Robespierre himself knelt beneath the guillotine. With his execution, the worst of the Terror ended.

The American minister, James Monroe, sought the release of heartbroken Madame de Lafayette. She was given better quarters, though still a prisoner; and finally she was set free on January 22, 1795. Her only wish now was for her and her daughters to join her husband in prison, and for young George Washington Lafayette to get out of the way of the enemies of his father. Adrienne arranged to send the fourteen-year-old boy to America, where he could be under the care of Washington.

His safety assured, she made an arduous trip to

Vienna, pretending to be an American woman. In Vienna, she sought out the Emperor Francis II.

"Let me share my husband's imprisonment, sire," she begged. "That is all I ask."

Eventually the Emperor agreed to give the heroic Adrienne, the boon she sought. At last on October 24, 1795, she and her two daughters looked from their carriage upon the towers of Olmutz.

For a year, ever since the attempt to escape prison, Lafayette had languished in solitary confinement at Olmutz. Surely he must have thought he had gone mad when the doors of his cell creaked open and he saw his beloved wife Adrienne and his daughters, Anastasie and Virginia. They fell weeping into each others' arms. The guards searched the luggage, clanked the doors behind the reunited family and left them to their happiness.

But their rejoicing was sadly marred by the news that Adrienne brought to her husband; for she told of the death of loved relatives and of some of his dearest friends and comrades, of his old enemy Orleans, and of the King and Queen whom he had sought to protect after helping to bring about the end of their despotic regime.

For nearly two years Adrienne and the girls shared their husband's and father's privations. At night the Marquis and Madame occupied a single cell; but each morning Madame de Lafayette was locked up with her daughters until noon. They joined the Marquis at dinner, and the family remained together until eight o'clock in the evening, when the girls were put back in their own cells. Not yet were they allowed knives and forks. Those

As the cell door opened, he saw his wife and daughters.

that Adrienne had brought were taken away. Through their small, high windows came the cries of soldiers being flogged, and always the air was filled with the dreadful stench. Lafayette was shoeless now, so out of an old corset of her mother's, Anastasie made shoes for her father.

During the winter, Madame de Lafayette almost died of what must have been scurvy brought on by an inadequate diet. After she recovered, the restrictions were slightly relaxed and their captors began treating them a little better. And by now they had found that their guards could be bribed. Secretly they corresponded with friends in the outside world. To their joy they learned that young George had reached America. He was not with Washington, but was living near New York and studying under a tutor in the home of a faithful friend, La Colombe, who had escaped to the United States.

In America Erich Bollman and Huger had gained an audience with the President. Thereupon Washington had written confidentially to the Emperor of Germany, seeking Lafayette's release. In England, too, friends of the Marquis urged his liberation.

But it was not the pleadings of Americans or Englishmen, or his return to the affections of the fickle French that brought about his release. Instead it was the growing shadow of a man whose name would be written large upon the pages of history. He was Napoleon Bonaparte, an Italian-blooded lieutenant from Corsica, who had displayed military genius and helped weld France into a united nation after the final throes of the Revolution. Now he was driving before him the enemies of France. And Bonaparte, as ordered by the five-man Directory which now governed France, demanded Lafayette's freedom. It was part of the price of a short-lived peace treaty. On September 19, 1797, five years and a month since Lafayette's flight from France had ended in imprisonment, the gates of Olmutz opened.

In time Napoleon would come to regret that he had won the release of the unyielding friend of freedom.

But Lafayette was not yet destined to return to France, though his homeland waited avidly to greet him despite its love for the newer hero Napoleon. Slowly the Lafayettes journeyed across the German countryside toward France. Once more the shouts of the multitude rang in their ears. But before they crossed the border, Lafayette learned that dictatorial force ruled his country once more.

Victorious under Napoleon against her outside enemies, France could not conquer her worst enemy, herself. Control of the nation, Lafayette learned, had been seized by three of the five-man Directory. With a legislative body of two assemblies, this Directory had been set up after the Reign of Terror to govern the nation. Behind the three Directors stood the bold, undemocratic Napoleon. Again representative government was dead.

This was old tyranny in new dress. Lafayette denounced the seizure of executive powers. He might have remained aloof. But he angrily refused to write to thank the Directory for his deliverance from prison. What the usurpers had done was not constitutional; and, as always, Lafayette was committed to government under law, which he had learned from the Americans.

The Directory refused to let him enter France. Now nearly forty years old, Lafayette was a man without a country. The fortune that once had made him one of the richest men in Europe was all but gone. He retired to the country home of

The figure of Napoleon cast a shadow over all France.

a kinswoman, the Countesse de Tesse, in Wittmold. There he began to write his recollections. It was a way to pay his debts and to get on his feet again.

To Wittmold came young George, home from America after six years. Now he was a sturdy young man of nineteen, the very age at which Lafayette had sailed on the *Victoire*. He bore a devoted letter from George Washington. The family joyfully celebrated the reunion. Then, desperate over his finances, the Marquis decided to go to America to regain his fortune among friends. But

France and America were now at odds, though not at war. It would not do to leave, for his presence in America could be embarrassing to his American friends and himself.

Forlornly, he sought refuge in the Batavian Republic, which was what Holland, then a vassal of France, was called. To seek even this refuge, Adrienne had to get official permission in Paris. So, while the armies of France battled throughout Europe, Lafayette, sick and disillusioned, turned to farming in Holland.

In Paris, his tireless wife pleaded with Napoleon Bonaparte in his behalf. Napoleon, no doubt recognizing in Lafayette an incorrupt and indomitable spirit, perhaps thought that he would need him. For even now the Corsican was planning to oust the Directory and seize all power. Lafayette wrote to Bonaparte, who answered in a friendly vein. And from Adrienne there came a passport under an assumed name and a message for him to re-enter France at once. The long exile was almost over.

9

NAPOLEON AND THE

BOURBONS AGAIN

What had held France together in the last appalling days of the Terror was the need to unite against her foreign foes or perish as a nation. Her sons had answered that need. Despite her internal torture France had thrown back the enemies beyond her borders: the fugitive Bourbon Royalists, the Austrians and the Prussians and their lesser allies. She had then turned to the attack.

The most brilliant military leader to emerge from this initial life-and-death struggle was Bonaparte. He had put down the final Parisian insurrections and had gone from the bloody streets of

Paris to the nation's embattled borders, and thence to the conquest of Italy. From then on his name would be spoken in anger, in fear, and in frenzied devotion throughout the world.

The Italian victory, coupled with the others, had given unbridled power to Napoleon. Overthrowing the Directory, he had become first consul of France. Then, intent on conquering England's Indian Empire, he overran Egypt, though he failed in his real purpose. Soon to the forces opposing Napoleon was added Russia. But he went his madly conquering way. He dreamed of possessing the world and he nearly did.

In 1804 Napoleon Bonaparte had himself made emperor. Overawed, Pope Pius VII took part in the coronation of this revolutionist as Emperor of France. Then Napoleon destroyed the old Holy Roman Empire.

Throughout Europe his kinsmen and favorites ruled vassal kingdoms. As fast as his enemies combined against him, Napoleon broke them up by his military victories. Only England held fast. Europe trembled before his triumphs. Those at Marengo, Hohenlinden, Ulm, Austerlitz and Jena were jewels in the imperial crown. Their battlefields be-

came the last resting places for tens of thousands
of the sons of France and Europe.

Seven times Europe combined against him. Six
times his enemies were defeated. The seventh alliance succeeded, but not before the best and bravest
of the Emperor's armies were destroyed. This followed his ill-fated invasion of Russia that ended
with the burning of Moscow and the disastrous
retreat of the French in the killing Russian winter.

On March 30, 1814, the Allies entered Paris.
Louis XVIII, brother of the guillotined king,
ascended the throne as the Allies' choice. Once
again a Bourbon ruled France. Napoleon was
shipped to the Island of Elba, an exile.

There still remained for him one hundred days
of glory before his final defeat. He escaped from
Elba and returned to France, where the people and
his old soldiers, already disgusted with the Bourbon restoration, flocked to his banners. Then came
the Battle of Waterloo when the English and
Prussians overwhelmed Napoleon's legions, on June
18, 1815. With that historic defeat, came his abdication. From then until long after Lafayette's
death, a Bourbon sat upon the throne of France.

And what of the Marquis in these momentous days?

He was to play at the last a noble and dominant role again; but not for long nor ever in behalf of Napoleon. Initially, after Madame de Lafayette had persuaded Bonaparte to permit her husband's return, the two strong-willed men got on well enough. Lafayette recognized the genius, the hypnotic qualities of leadership and the courage of Napoleon. He also saw in the Corsican adventurer the ruthless tyrant, the ruler to whom constitutional rights would mean no more than to a Bourbon. Bonaparte in turn recognized in Lafayette a man whose iron will matched his own, whose sense of morality was far greater than his, and whose popularity and devotion to France could be useful weapons in Napoleon's hands. He sought to win Lafayette to his side.

Bonaparte was then first consul, having already seized control from the dictatorial three-man Directory. The Marquis could have had any post within Napoleon's power, which meant anything in France. But he turned down even the ministership to the United States, saying that he would not go to his loved adopted country in other than an American uniform. To an offer of a seat in Napoleon's hand-picked Senate, he answered, "I should be obliged the next day to denounce the government and its chief."

When Napoleon demanded an explanation of his unfriendly behavior, he answered, "If Bonaparte had been willing to serve the cause of liberty, I should have been devoted to him. But I can neither approve an arbitrary government nor associate myself with it."

No one else in all Europe would have dared to talk thus to or about Napoleon. But the conquerer at first seemed to enjoy Lafayette's criticism. The two spent long hours together, discussing their respective views.

Finally the break came, as it had to. The enraged Bonaparte told Lafayette that his criticism of Bonaparte's acts aided the enemies of France. Lafayette reminded Napoleon that he was living in retirement and that he avoided all occasions to speak. This was true enough.

"But, General, if anyone asks me if your regime conforms to my ideas of liberty, I shall reply, 'No'," he said in stubborn honesty. "In a word, General,

I should like very much to be prudent, but I will not be a renegade."

Thus came the inevitable enmity. To one antagonist—Lafayette—liberty and honor were paramount. To the other—Napoleon—power and world conquest were all that mattered.

Earlier Lafayette had urged upon Bonaparte the simplicity of the American form of government, with an elected house and senate and a president responsible to the people. Napoleon had replied angrily, "That sort of thing wouldn't go in France."

There was one notable difference between Bonaparte and the Bourbons he had supplanted. Lafayette did not pay with his life as so many did who had stood up against the tyrant kings.

Instead, Lafayette and his family retired in disgrace to the beautiful chateau of La Grange, forty miles from Paris, an inheritance of Adrienne and almost all that was left to the family. He had lost nearly everything of his own. La Grange was one of the de Noailles estates which Adrienne had received in the division of what remained to her family after the revolution.

For the next several years the Lafayette family spent their time in pursuits far removed from the turmoil of war and politics. Adrienne—Madame de Lafayette, we should now call her—set about trying to find the graves of her murdered mother and sister and grandmother. Finally she discovered where they were buried. They were three among many victims of the guillotine who had been interred in long, deep pits at Picpus, near the Bastille.

But the Lafayettes knew happiness too. They rejoiced in the marriage of George, in June, 1802, to Emilie de Tracy, the daughter of an old colleague and comrade-in-arms of Lafayette, and sharer of his ideals. They delighted, too, in the marriage of Virginia to Louis de Lasteyre du Saillante, a liberal-minded young member of the old nobility. Their first daughter, Anastasie, had already been wed to the son of the General's close friend and fellow prisoner, Charles de la Tour-Maubourg.

At La Grange, Lafayette entertained the great Whig leader of England, Charles Fox, whom he had long admired and who had been chief among the Englishmen seeking his freedom. When, in a conversation, Lafayette mourned the death of liberty, Fox replied, "Liberty will come to life again, but not for us; for George (your son) at the earliest, and surely for his children." He was right.

In February of 1803, the forty-six-year-old Lafayette suffered a crippling accident. He slipped on the ice while visiting in Paris and broke his left leg. Permitting a new treatment, the stretching of the broken limbs by what was called the Boyer machine, he suffered gangrene. Though the leg was saved, the hip was permanently stiffened. For the rest of his life he limped.

Meanwhile, the gallant soldier had not been forgotten by his loved America. From President Jefferson came a letter offering him an appointment as governor of the new Louisiana Territory, which the Americans had so wisely purchased from Napoleon for almost nothing—$15,000,000. Congress assigned to him 11,540 acres along the banks of the Ohio.

The American President wrote that he had set this grant aside and had secured for him much more valuable land in Louisiana. Lafayette had just accepted the latter grant, through an agent in Louisiana, when Congress ceded the tract to the City of New Orleans. He could have kept it; but he abandoned all claim for the tremendous acreage which could have enriched him and his heirs for all time to come.

Now Napoleon—ruler of the French empire by his action in May of 1804—renewed his attempts to win over Lafayette. But the proud, unchanging rebel against all dictators refused an offer of the coveted Legion of Honor with a contemptuous comment. Again he refused also a seat in the senate.

The General was enjoying now the quiet, unmilitary country life at La Grange. He delighted in agricultural experiments. His lands were highly productive. He had developed rare flocks of sheep and herds of cattle. The cider from his presses had become the regional drink. Unlike so many great estates, La Grange was paying its way and helping to take care of the family.

It was just as well that this was so. La Grange was a mecca for many hundreds of visitors— Americans on tour, fugitives from the wrath of Napoleon, outspoken philosophers, old comrades-in-arms and many another.

The General was kind to his tenants, even when they stole from him. When they were caught, he secretly paid their fines. In hard times, he gave away soup and bread to hundreds upon hundreds. A peasant who had fallen and broken his leg while stealing wood was sent at his expense to Paris for treatment.

Only infrequently did he go to Paris. But his friends kept him informed; and constantly he wrote to Jefferson and others of his American comrades.

Lafayette's self-imposed withdrawal from the French scene was violated by Napoleon's hatred. Young George Washington Lafayette, his son, had entered the army early. So had Anastasie's husband, who was the son of his friend La Tour-Marbourg. But so intense was the Emperor's wrath against Lafayette that George, despite three wounds in defense of the Empire, and a brilliant career in the early Napoleonic wars, was refused promotion time and again. His brother-in-law received no better treatment. Finally, in despair, they resigned.

Quietly—so he supposed—Lafayette prepared to live out the rest of his life in retirement at the beautiful chateau of La Grange. His tranquility was tragically disturbed late in the summer of 1807. Madame was felled by a return of the illness which she had suffered as Lafayette's companion in prison at Olmutz. In vain, trips were undertaken for her health. Lafayette was at Chavaniac, the old family home, when something told him to return to La Grange. His fears were well founded, even though Adrienne was better on his arrival. The General never left her alone although she begged him to attend to his many interests.

"I have no affairs," he said, "other than to care for you."

Gradually Adrienne grew more ill. In her delirium she talked constantly of her beloved husband and of her children and grandchildren. She wandered on about Lafayette's reforms in behalf of democracy, and about his religious beliefs which she did not feel were strong enough. Lafayette suffered greatly, for he reproved himself inwardly for his desertions of Adrienne in liberty's behalf.

His consolation came one evening just before her death.

"How happy I have been!" she exclaimed. "What a role to be your wife!"

On Christmas Eve, she died. Her last words to him were: "I am all yours." So ended an extraordinary marriage.

Lafayette would live twenty-seven more years, but life had lost much of its meaning. In fact he was pleased that seemingly he was forgotten politically in France. His old world, like his family happiness, was dead. The new empire itself, built by the dread Emperor but nevertheless the Empire of France, was falling to pieces. Seven years after the death of Adrienne, the Allies were driving on Paris. When the Prussians and Austrians and their cohorts entered Paris on the thirty-first of March, 1814, Lafayette locked himself in his rooms and gave way to uncontrollable tears, not for the defeat of Napoleon but for the conquest of France.

Now, with the seeming end of the Napoleonic regime, the Bourbons swarmed into Paris. Trying to make the best of things, Lafayette, the Emperor's enemy, went to court. Louis XVIII was gracious enough. But the returned members of the nobility were unforgiving. They spurned Lafayette. The defeated Frenchmen who had followed Napoleon turned their own backs on the Bourbons and the satellites, who behaved more like Spaniards and Germans and Prussians than Frenchmen. As usual Lafayette was in the middle. In that winter of the Allied victory, the English Duke of Wellington, whose greatest role was still ahead of him, met Lafayette at a party. They did not get along well together.

Soon Lafayette returned to La Grange. He was no less hated by the returning Bourbons than by the minions of Napoleon with whom he had never made a truce.

Vigorously he denounced the Royalists who were mocking him. His only pleasure was in the victory of Andrew Jackson over the British at New Orleans in January, 1815, and the suppression of the slave traffic in Europe and wherever else the Congress of Vienna could act.

And then came word that Napoleon had escaped from Elba and was on his way to Paris.

At once Lafayette set out for Paris. He was there when Napoleon arrived, only a few hours after the terrified Louis XVIII had fled. But Lafayette had little confidence in this new Napoleon, despite the former Emperor's frenzied attempts at democratic declarations. In vain, his friends and the friends of Napoleon begged him to side with the returned Emperor. War was inevitable again. The Allies, under Britain's Wellington, were determined to crush the returned Bonaparte.

Lafayette demanded that Napoleon assemble elected representatives of the people and thus institute a truely democratic government. He refused the Emperor's offer of a high peerage, and he did not trust Napoleon's asserted belief in democracy.

In this grave crisis Lafayette was elected a deputy to the French Assembly. He did not want the office, but he felt that he could not refuse. And so, after twenty-three years, he found himself, an aging man, involved again in the fate of France.

Once more Napoleon sought to win Lafayette to his side. He could not. On June 12th the Emperor led his army into Belgium. There at Waterloo France went down in irreparable defeat before the might of England and Prussia. In eight days Bonaparte was back in Paris. With the Battle of Waterloo lost, Napoleon was determined to end representative rule in France, become dictator, and somehow fight on.

But once more in prostrate France, the voice of

Lafayette, urging order and constitutional government, prevailed. In the Chamber of Deputies he won approval of a resolution declaring the Chamber in permanent session. Any attempt to end its actions would be considered a treasonable crime. That would cripple Napoleon. Lafayette urged and won support for a demand for the abdication of the Emperor himself. Here Napoleon's final downfall was accomplished. Somehow, in their moment of full defeat, the people of France accepted, through their representatives, a government of constitutional law. Lafayette's dream had triumphed.

At first Napoleon refused to give way. But Lafayette sent an ultimatum to him.

"If the Emperor does not send in his abdication within an hour," he declared, "I will propose to the Chamber that he be dethroned."

Napoleon resigned, speechless with rage and despair. Despite Lafayette's suggestion that he seek refuge in the United States, he surrendered to the British. His captors dispatched him to the island of St. Helena where he would spend the rest of his life

The abdication of Napoleon did not mean a triumph for democracy. Once more the home-grown enemies of freedom took over France. Lafayette was omitted from the Directorate, for both the followers of Bonaparte and the rebellious Republicans hated him. The Assembly ordered him to seek out the commanders of the Allied powers and persuade them to end their march upon Paris. Lafayette tried to find and halt them. And of course he failed. No one could have stopped that victorious advance. Napoleon's France must be humiliated. Soon the puppet flag of the Bourbons flew over Paris; Prussian troops ran rampant through the city; and the hated British were everywhere.

In Paris on September 26, 1815, Russia, Austria and Prussia formed what they called the Holy Alliance. They pledged themselves to the defense of the divine right of kings, and to the crushing of religious liberty and all democracies. This was the Alliance which President James Monroe of the young American Republic would answer defiantly with the Monroe Doctrine. In effect, it would tell Europe's kings, "Stay out of the New World!"

Once more Lafayette returned to the haven of La Grange. Despite all he had endured, he was still a strong and healthy man, though he walked with a limp because of his injured hip. Much of his time he spent corresponding with his many friends, the friends of liberty throughout the world. The cause of freedom became his religion. Each day he paid lonely homage to his departed Adrienne. He was host to countless visitors. He was beloved by the poor of his countryside because of his many kindnesses.

But the old revolutionary could not continue his quiet life for long. He kept one eye on Paris where the behavior of the restored Bourbons was not to his liking. He determined to return to political life.

Soon he re-entered the Chamber of Deputies. His election frightened many a rotten aristocrat and noble. Everywhere it was whispered that Lafayette's return to active politics would mean another revolution. And again, as he took his seat in the Chamber of Deputies, he became an idol of the multitude. But not of the Royalists! As he spoke publicly for the first time in many years, on the twenty-second of March, 1819, the members and his audience alike could almost feel the wave of hate that swept toward him from his Royalist enemies. What he talked about was as basic to Americans as life itself—the right of the taxpayer to vote, the need for freedom of the press, and the meaning of personal liberty to the citizen of a free country. This represented almost everything that the triumphant Royalists feared. And they hated Lafayette all the more because in him they saw a traitor to his own class.

The ringing words of Lafayette did not triumph over the forces of reaction. The free press and individual liberty were suppressed. It was even proposed that each noble and other large landowner should cast not one vote but many, in proportion to what each owned.

Again the outraged Lafayette turned revolutionist in the full sense. First he organized a revolutionary society "The Friends of the Liberty of the Press." The members plotted to overthrow the government. Nine of his fellow plotters were jailed, but Lafayette went untouched. The Royalists did not dare to arrest him.

On May 27, he thundered in the Assembly his greatest speech—a declaration of the right of man to self-government. He demanded that each citizen receive his "independent right and duty" to vote. The Assembly was almost transformed into a mob as his enemies spat out their hatred of him. But basically all he was doing was, in his own words, seeking "the national, constitutional and peaceable path—the path of good will."

To President Monroe he wrote at this time that the idea of freedom was everywhere in ferment. He added hopefully that the new generation would support those pure ideals. He would not live to see that day dawn in France. But it was not far away.

We must remember that everywhere the common man of Europe was struggling for liberty—in Spain and Portugal, in Greece and Italy and Germany, and also in the New World's South America.

No wonder then that Lafayette was attracted to a new secret society, the Carbonari, even though his more careful friends urged him not to join. The Carbonari in France was much like another society of the same name that was battling for Italian freedom. Lafayette and his hot-headed young friends now plotted a forcible overthrow of the Bourbon king. Meanwhile he raged on in the Assembly. Although admitting the terrible wrongs of the revolution of 1789, he said, "It was the victory of right over privilege; the revolution was the emancipation and the development of human faculties, the restoration of the people to power."

Meanwhile, Napoleon had died at St. Helena. The old Bonaparte followers, being arrayed against the Bourbons, sought to join forces with Lafayette's reckless liberals. Throughout France the people were now despairing of gaining freedom by peaceful means. The nation was wracked by religious and political persecution.

Soon the old General was the leader of the Carbonari, perhaps 40,000 strong. He was ideal for the cause; for he was fearless, without ambition, already a hero of the people, and with little to live for that he had not already won.

Lafayette and his fellow conspirators plotted a forcible overthrow of the Bourbon king and the establishment of a revolutionary government. Carefully selected officers and troops awaited the order to revolt. But the plot was discovered the day after Lafayette had spent many hours, on Christmas Eve, at the shrine of his wife. The planned uprisings fizzled out. Some of the ringleaders paid with their lives for the ill-fated revolution. Lafayette was forced to seek refuge for a while in the American legation. There he schemed without success to free his imprisoned fellow conspirators.

But his enemies failed to prove that he had

taken part in the Carbonari revolt. In November, 1822, he was again elected to the Assembly. Now he was shadowed continuously by Bourbon spies, but he continued to plot the overthrow of the King. Lafayette was engaged in a losing fight. In February of 1824, when he sought re-election to the Assembly, he was defeated. The money and lies of the agents of the Bourbons and the unjust new law which gave the rich far more votes than the poor were too much for him.

And once again the lonely and seemingly defeated man went back to La Grange. At sixty-seven, he had little left but his memories.

10

AMERICA AND
JOURNEY'S END

This was the spring of 1824. Lafayette, aging and despairing of democracy in Europe, was shadowed by the spies of the Bourbons. He thought longingly of the United States where the torch of liberty still burned brightly. Heartsick, he yearned to visit America again.

There came to him then, like a heaven-sent gift, a letter from President Monroe and from other and older Americans. These were the friends of his youth—among them the aged Jefferson—urging him to visit the nation which loved him.

That spring Congress issued an official invitation

to him and placed at his disposal an American frigate.

Joyfully Lafayette accepted the invitation but declined the use of the American man-of-war. With his son, George Washington, and his secretary and manservant, he embarked in July for his final journey to America.

Now, as in 1777, he was plagued by Bourbon autocracy. The government would allow no procession or demonstration in his honor as he embarked. Troops even broke up a parade to his departing ship.

A month later, in August, he saw the trees and trim white houses of Staten Island in the bay of New York. At an incredibly far distance he heard the wild shouting of his beloved Americans. Fort Lafayette fired in salute. For a while his eyes were blinded with tears. Alongside his ship, the *Cadmus*, sped the first steamboat he had ever seen. But the day was Sunday and the religious Americans of New York deferred until the next day their truly thunderous reception.

Never before and never since has the United States given to any man such a welcome as this one which began in New York and lasted through his long happy visit.

Cannon thundered, and the band from West Point played "The Marseillaise," which Lafayette hadn't heard publicly in France since the Bourbons had returned to power. Aging veterans of the Revolution crowded about him. As he disembarked, Lafayette burst into uncontrollable tears.

Beside him marched the "Guards of Lafayette," each wearing on his chest a portrait of the old Marquis. The militiamen wore ribbons lettered "Welcome Lafayette." As the procession wended up Broadway he was half-hidden by flowers thrown upon him. For two hours each day, for four days, he met all comers at receptions in the City Hall.

Each day a fete and each night a banquet were held in his honor. He shook hands with tens of thousands of shouting, crying Americans.

The driver of a coach said lovingly to one of the horses, "Behave pretty now, Charlie, behave pretty. You are going to carry the greatest man in the world."

Lafayette traveled by day and night, and always there awaited him torch-bearing cavalrymen and cheering Americans who remembered the old, heroic days.

Massachusetts sought to outdo New York. At Roxbury there paraded his own Light Infantry in their familiar red and black plumes. This exhibition moved him more greatly than anything else on his visit. He was wined and dined prodigiously. At one Massachusetts breakfast he ate a canvasback duck, six perch, a plate of hominy and a glass of Bordeaux wine.

Complimented by the Massachusetts Senate on his English-speaking ability, he replied proudly: "Why should I not, being an American just returned from a long visit to Europe?"

Every American city he visited tried to outdo the other. In Philadelphia huge carnival floats paraded in the streets. Lafayette's triumphal procession was halted by the American guides on the very spot where he and de Kalb and their companions had been so rudely treated when they first presented themselves. For hours he stood in the hall where the Declaration of Independence was signed, his right hand swollen and bruised from the handclasps of the thousands who filed past him.

For a week he endured gladly a daily reception in Independence Hall and every night a banquet.

In Hartford his birthday was celebrated by a banquet of the Society of the Cincinnati.

In Washington, the new capital of the United States, Lafayette was delighted that he found "no sentinels, no guards, not even a valet." He was welcomed by President Monroe; and here he met Andrew Jackson, who had defeated the old foe, Great Britain, at the battle of New Orleans ten years before. Lafayette and Jackson became fast friends.

Curiously, the bitterness of the presidential campaign then being waged faded before the nation's adulation of their French hero. Young America was reliving its past in the person of this sturdy old man, a little stout now and wearing a wig. The French Minister, instructed by the resentful Bourbons to take no part in honoring him, refused to join in the acclamation. This didn't bother the Americans. They disliked royalty and its pretensions as much as did their visitor.

His saddest day of the tour came when he visited the tomb of the man who had been father and commander and spiritual guide. Once again he

In every city Lafayette was cheered by throngs of people.

wept as, with his son and his secretary, he entered
the first President's sarcophagus. George Washington Custis, the President's stepson, presented him
a ring with these words: "Will you never tire in
the cause for freedom and human happiness! Surely
where liberty dwells, there must be the country of
Lafayette."

Bands played, and children threw flowers before their hero.

And so on and on he journeyed in triumphant procession: to Yorktown, where long ago he had forced the surrender of Cornwallis; to Richmond; and to Monticello. There the impatient 81-year-old Jefferson waited to greet him. Lafayette could hardly recognize the old statesman, now bent and weakened, dressed in the clothing of a half-century past, but enthusiastic in his greeting, eager to talk of the old, crowded days. A more vigorous former President, James Madison, now seventy-four, rode horseback beside Lafayette's coach for many miles, after the Marquis ended a four-day visit with him.

Tired out at last, Lafayette settled down for the winter in Gadsby's Hotel in Washington. In December he spoke before a joint meeting of the Senate and House, with the galleries crowded with 2,000 listeners. He heard himself praised by Henry Clay. And Congress, aware that he had lost almost all his fortune in liberty's behalf, appropriated for him $200,000 and a township of public land. The states of Virginia, Maryland and New York wished likewise to reward him, but the Marquis refused.

"I think the American nation has already done too much for me," he said.

In February he was rested enough to tour the South and West. This was a journey of 4,000 miles by carriage over bad roads and through frontier wilderness. He went to Raleigh and Fayetteville in North Carolina, the state through which he had traveled on his first rigorous journey to Philadelphia. On he went to Camden in South Carolina, where the heroic de Kalb had died; to Columbia and Charleston, to Savannah and Augusta in Georgia; and to New Orleans whose predominantly French population met him with open arms.

Only one practice in his beloved United States outraged him. This was the enslavement of the Negro, so widespread throughout the South. In New Orleans he warmly received a group of free Negroes who had fought in 1815 under Andrew Jackson in the Battle of New Orleans. The indirect protest was not lost on his audience.

He went on to Baton Rouge and Natchez and on up-river to old St. Louis, a tiny town of only 6,000 people. At Kaskaskia, Illinois, he was welcomed by descendants of French Canadians; and at Nashville, Tennessee, Andrew Jackson himself met him at the river front and entertained him at a magnificent dinner in his gracious home, The Hermitage.

His steamboat hit a snag and sank in the Ohio, taking with it 600 unanswered letters, which must have pleased him, because he was woefully behind in his correspondence.

At Cincinnati the redoubtable warrior, General Harrison, old Tippecanoe himself, praised him as the companion of Washington, the friend of Franklin and Adams and Jefferson, and the devoted champion of liberty. In Ohio Lafayette described Cincinnati as the most cultured city of the West, and the state as the eighth wonder of the world.

From Cincinnati the triumphal procession continued to Wheeling and Uniontown, Erie, Dunkirk, Fredonia, Buffalo, Niagara Falls and Fort Niagara, Syracuse and Utica, where Lafayette gave presents to three Indian chiefs who had served under him; then Schenectady, Albany and thence to Boston, just two days before the celebration of the Battle of Bunker Hill.

Seven thousand veterans, regular troops, and members of patriotic organizations marched in his honor in the Bunker Hill ceremony while 200,000 cheering citizens lined the highways. As a member of the Masonic order, Lafayette laid the cornerstone of the Bunker Hill Monument with a silver trowel. There he heard Daniel Webster declaim that through Lafayette "heaven saw fit to ordain that the electric spark of liberty should be conducted from the New World to the old."

That evening the old hero sat at dinner with 4,000 persons in a great, rough barracks. He

answered the toast of his welcomers with a re-
sponse "to Bunker Hill and the holy resistance to
oppression which has already enfranchised the
American hemisphere. The next half century's
jubilee shall be to enfranchised Europe."

Almost everywhere in the New World he traveled
with a vigor that would have been surprising in
a far younger man. He talked with the old Revolutionist, John Adams. He was feted in New
Hampshire and Maine and Vermont. Retracing his
steps, he arrived in New York on the morning of
July 3rd, and there he kissed a six-year-old boy
whom later generations would know as the poet
Walt Whitman.

At Brandywine Creek in Pennsylvania, he pointed
out where the Colonials had crossed the turgid
stream before the battle in which he had been
wounded. Once more he visited Monroe and
Madison and the enfeebled Jefferson; and at the
urging of his friends he delayed his departure
until after his own sixty-ninth birthday on September 6th. The birthday was celebrated at the
White House. There the President, in violation of
an established custom, drank a toast to him; and

John Quincy Adams hailed alike the twenty-second of February and the sixth of September, the birthday of Washington and the birthday of Lafayette.

Finally came the day of departure. It was a day of mourning in America and of sadness in the old fighter's heart. As the frigate which bore him sailed past Mount Vernon, Lafayette doffed his hat. For long minutes he gazed, misty-eyed, at the home of Washington until it passed from view. Save in his heart, he would know his loved America no more.

What a contrast was his return to oppressed France! Outside the home of a friend the people sought to hail him. But as he answered their serenade by appearing on the balcony, Royal Guards and gendarmes rode roughshod into the gathering, wounding and arresting men and women and children. Nevertheless the people of France persisted in hailing him.

Even now Lafayette was no man to live out his life only with his memories, though he knew that few years remained. Jefferson and Adams had died on the same day, the fourth of July, just fifty years after the signing of the Declaration of Independence, which had been so largely theirs. Lafayette had no time to waste. Once again he entered political life, becoming a deputy from the city of Meaux in the Chamber of Deputies.

In 1827 the liberal wing of French politics won a resounding victory and gained a majority in the new Chamber of Deputies. Once more the seventy-year-old survivor of war and revolution, imprisonment and persecution, became the center of progressive French thought.

To one and all who came to his salon, the General preached political freedom. In the Chamber of Deputies he fought for wider education and for reforms far ahead of his time. He sought these goals in a country which politically, morally and socially was extremely backward.

The harsh spirit of the Bourbons would not die. On July 27th the King suspended the freedom of the press, ended by royal order the session of the Chamber of Deputies, and in many other ways took away what liberties the French had clung to.

And so in 1830, for the last time the old revolutionist conspired and rose against tyranny. Fighting broke out and Lafayette's arrest was sought. Yet his enemies planned to have him made once more the commander of the National Guard. They believed that with Lafayette as the figurehead of a revolutionary government they could betray him later. He agreed to accept the post. But he was less impetuous now. He sought for France only a limited monarchy, with a King who could be restrained by a constitution and the elected representatives of the people; and so he supported Louis Philippe as successor to the hated Louis XVIII. Louis Philippe was the son of his ancient enemy, the Duke d' Orleans. Lafayette drew up notable demands which included wider voting privileges, the end of hereditary peerage of the nobility, and popular city and regional elections. The reviled monarch gave in.

Again Lafayette had helped win a revolution. The new King named him commander in chief of the National Guard. On August 29, 1830, as he had done so many years ago, Lafayette reviewed his Guardsmen. And once more he fought the terrible mob of Paris, seeking now the death of the hated ministers of the old King.

We cannot explore now the twistings and turnings of French politics and the movement of the French nation toward eventual democracy in the

last years of Lafayette's life. All we need to remember is that France again was torn by dissen-
tion, not the terrible bloodletting of the old days
of the commune but still a death struggle of king
against the rights of ordinary men.

By 1831 France was again near anarchy.
Lafayette, almost seventy-five, continued to oppose
the new King, whom he had helped put on the
throne. Although he was a likable family man,
Louis Philippe had gone back on his promises to
the people.

Once more, in 1832, Lafayette heard the howl-
ing of the mob. Louis Philippe became ever more
unpopular. On the heels of a terrible cholera plague
in Paris, leaders of the mob demanded the King's
abolition and urged Lafayette to form a republic.
But Lafayette knew the mob of old. He refused
to lead it. The Dragoons of the King dispersed
the clamoring people in the Place de la Bastille.
Bloody fighting raged in Paris, but this time the
Bourbons remained in power.

Through these dismal times, the old rebel never
gave up. In the Chamber he still bespoke the cause
of liberalism, and predicted the triumph of the
Republican cause which he would not live to wit-

ness. In May of 1834, drenched in a storm, he fell ill. Hopelessly stricken, he smiled grimly in bed at the premature report in the Paris newspapers of his death.

As his life sands began to run out, Lafayette said to members of his family: "Life is like the flame of a lamp. When there is no more oil—pouf! It goes out and it is all over." At dawn on May 20th, it was all over. His last act was to press to his lips a locket holding a miniature and lock of hair of his beloved, long-dead Adrienne.

Even in death the Bourbons feared Lafayette. Demonstrations and funeral orations were forbidden. He was buried beside Adrienne and her own loved ones in Picpus, near a secluded walled garden and not far from where the Bastille had once frowned down on the people.

Royal France refused to bury Lafayette with military honors. But in America, a month after his death, President Jackson ordered the same military rites that had been accorded after the death of Washington himself. The Stars and Stripes hung at half-mast throughout the United States. All army and navy officers wore mourning bands for six months and the members of Congress themselves went into mourning. The American man-of-war, *Brandywine*, brought over earth from Bunker Hill to surround the casket of Lafayette.

America did not forget in 1834. And America still remembers the young Marquis. He was one of the authors of our liberty, and a tireless fighter for the yet unwon freedom of all mankind. An aristocrat, a man of wealth, he was born on the side of the rulers and not the ruled. Nevertheless he had striven all his life for political freedom, for the rights of the little man and for such privileges as freedom of the press, the suppression of privileged orders, the end of arbitrary imprisonment by royal edict, religious toleration and popular representation, trial by jury and the freedom of slaves. America had inspired him, the America which spoke in Jefferson's Declaration of Independence. The story that he had heard first as a teen-age officer in Metz illumined his mind and glowed in his heart.

Many have been his epitaphs. But nothing is more fitting to remember him by than a toast which was drunk to him by President James Monroe, and the answer he prophetically made.

Here is the way Lafayette, the friend of freedom, was described by the President of the United States:

"To the great apostle of liberty whom the persecutions of tyranny could not defeat, whom the love of riches could not influence, whom popular applause could never seduce! He was always the same, in the shackles of Olmutz, in his various labors, on the summits of power and glory."

And here was Lafayette's answering toast:

"To the perpetual union of the United States! It has already saved us in times of storm. One day it will save the world."

INDEX

Adams, John, 169–70
Adams, Samuel, 67
American Revolution, arms obtained in Europe, 15
and French alliance, 49–52
low ebb of, 42*ff*., 61–62, 66*ff*.
victorious end of, 76
André, John, 62, 64–65
Arnold, Benedict, 62–64, 67–69
Assembly of Notables, in France, 87–88
Austrians, 110, 113–14, 116–17, 138, 149, 153

Bastille, 89, 92–93, 99, 101, 107
Bay of Biscay, 3, 20, 55
Blockade of French fleet, 65–66
Bollman, Justus Erich, 124–27, 129, 133
Bourbons, 9, 11, 83, 138, 174
restored to throne of France, 140, 149–50, 154, 156–58, 171
Brandywine Creek, 39*ff*., 169
British Army, qualities of, 37
Bunker Hill Monument, 168–69
Burgoyne, John, 46–47

Camden, S. C., 35, 62, 166
Carbonari revolt, 156–58
Carolinas, American defeats in, 62, 66, 68
Chamber of Deputies, in France, 152, 154, 171

Charleston, S. C., 21–24, 62, 75, 125, 166
Chavaniac, France, 6, 79, 107–08, 121, 148
Clinton, Henry, 46, 53, 66, 68
Commune, in Paris, 104
Congress, Continental, 26–29, 56, 58–59, 66–67, 73
Congress of Vienna, 150
Continental Army, casualties of, 41–42, 62
discipline lacking in, 37
fighting qualities of, 38
hardships of, 45–46, 62
and Lafayette, as commander 44–45
as major general, 17–18, 27–29
ragged appearance of, 33, 36–37
reduced strength of, 46, 61
at Valley Forge, 42–46, 48
Conway, Thomas, 47, 49
Cornwallis, Lord, 43, 62, 66, 68–73
surrender of, 73–75, 165
Custis, George Washington, 164

Danton, 110, 115, 129
d'Ayen, Duke, 9–11, 17
Deane, Silas, 16–17
Declaration of Independence, 15, 67, 79, 92, 162, 170–71, 175
de Grasse, Admiral, 70–71